A&C BLACK • GUITAR

Abracadabra SINGALONG GUITAR

Learn to strum and sing your favourite songs

CD track list

CD 1

01 Tuning track
02 Row, row, row your boat
03 Row, row, row you boat backing
04 Ten in a bed
05 Ten in the bed backing
06 He's got the whole world in his hands
07 He's got the whole world in his hands backing
08 London's burning
09 London's burning backing
10 Silent night
11 Silent night backing
12 Frere Jacques
13 Frere Jacques backing
14 She'll be coming round the mountain
15 She'll be coming round the mountain backing
16 What will we do with the drunken sailor?
17 What will we do with the drunken sailor? backing
18 Away in a manger
19 Away in a manger backing
20 Wild thing
21 Wild thing backing
22 Little brown jug
23 Little brown jug backing
24 Rock around the clock
25 Rock around the clock backing

CD 2

01 Tuning track
02 The animals went in two by two
03 The animals went in two by two backing
04 Amazing grace
05 Amazing grace backing
06 You really got me
07 You really got me backing
08 Scarborough Fayre
09 Scarborough Fayre backing
10 Head, shoulders knees and toes
11 Head, shoulders knees and toes backing
12 If you're happy and you know it
13 If you're happy and you know it backing
14 Jingle bells
15 Jingle bells backing
16 Oh when the saints
17 Oh when the saints backing
18 You are my sunshine
19 You are my sunshine backing
20 House of the rising sun
21 House of the rising sun backing
22 Daisy Bell
23 Daisy Bell backing
24 My Bonnie lies over the ocean
25 My Bonnie lies over the ocean backing
26 I can see clearly now the rain is gone
27 I can see clearly now the rain is gone backing

Contents

2 **CD track list**
3 **Contents**

Introductory pages

4 Lyrics, chords and rhythm
4 Three steps to success
4 All together now
4 The guitar

5 Buying, care, holding the guitar
5 What are notes? Open strings
6 Tuning the guitar, how to play notes
6 Left hand position, chords
7 Chords (cont), when to strum
7 Left hand position, chords

8 **A major and E major chords**

9 Row, row, row your boat
10 Ten in a bed
12 He's got the whole world in his hands

14 **D major and G major chords**
15 London's burning
16 Silent night

18 **C major, A minor and E minor chords**

19 Frere Jacques
20 She'll be coming round the mountain
22 What will we do with the drunken sailor?
24 Away in a manger
26 Wild thing
28 Little brown jug
30 Rock around the clock
32 The animals went in two by two
34 Amazing Grace
36 You really got me
38 Scarborough Fayre

40 **A7, D7 chords**
41 **F major chord (barring)**

42 Head shoulders knees and toes
44 If you're happy and you know it
46 Jingle bells
48 Oh when the saints
50 You are my sunshine
52 House of the rising sun

54 **B7 and D minor chords**

55 Daisy Bell
58 My Bonnie lies over the ocean
60 I can see clearly now the rain is gone

62 **Melody lines**

71 **Index of chord diagrams**

Back cover **Acknowledgements**

Introduction

Abracadabra Singalong Guitar is a must-have for budding or experienced guitarists. It is a collection of popular songs and chords suitable for playing in groups, with singers or alone.
You do not have to read music, and there is no notation in the main part of the book. However, if you can read music, there are melody lines on pages 62 - 70, and a chord index on page 71.
Abracadabra Singalong guitar includes two CDs. Each song has two tracks; a performance track (with vocals) and a backing track (without vocals).

Lyrics, chords and rhythm

All lyric pages can be photocopied as many times as necessary.

Above the lyrics are large chord letters such as **A** or **E** and at the top of the page is a 'Chords used in this song' section, which has large versions of the chord diagrams. You will find full explanations of individual chords throughout the book (see contents page).
Ideally you should strum every time you see a chord letter above the lyrics. If you want to strum less or more that's fine. Aim to strum a rhythm that feels comfortable. Listen to the backing track and copy how the guitarist is playing the chords.

Three steps to success

The first half of the activities page focuses on the guitar. It is an easy three-step guide to tackling the song. Often it will urge you to revise the chords used, and will give you tips on the most effective way to learn and play the song.

All together now

Abracadabra Singalong Guitar is a resource for individual or group players. The 'All together now' section offers advice on performing the song in a group. Here there are ideas for extra vocal and guitar parts, tuned and untuned percussion parts, and related classroom activites - therefore those who do not even play the guitar can join in with the performance.
The songs can make fantastic group performances by a class, a choir, in assemblies or by guitar groups.

The Guitar

There are many types of guitar available, both electric and non-amplified.
It is advisable to begin learning with the classical guitar rather than acoustic or electric. For the beginner, the nylon strings on the classical are far less tiring to play than steel strings.

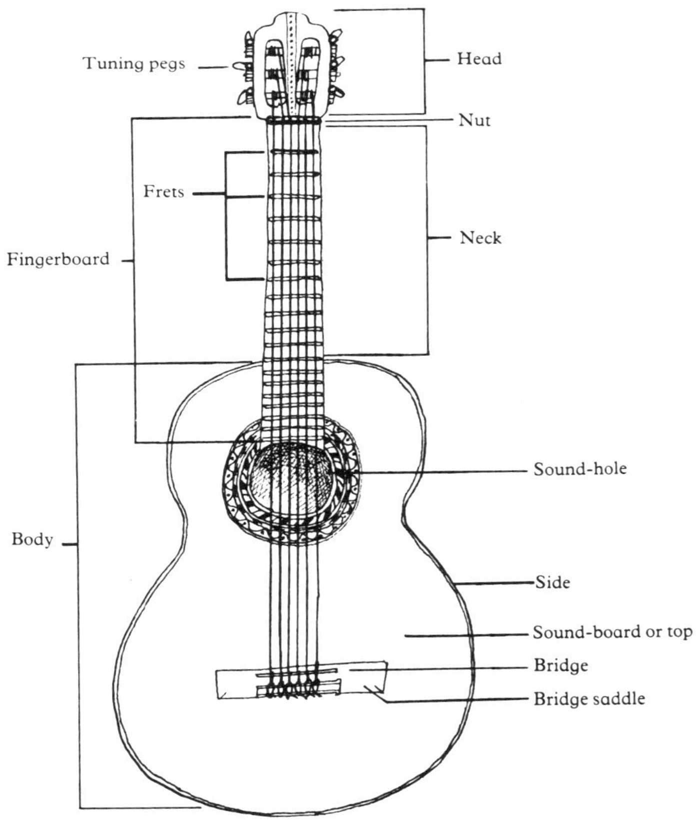

NEVER PUT STEEL STRINGS ON A CLASSICAL GUITAR.

Buying

Here are some of the things that you should check when buying a guitar:

- Make sure that the neck is straight and that the body does not move at the neck joint.
- Check that the bridge and bridge-saddle are securely attached to the body.
- Make sure that the tuning pegs are easy to turn with a little firm pressure of the fingers, and yet are firm enough not to slip.
- If possible ask someone who has experience of instruments to help you choose.

Care

- Do not expose your guitar to extremes of heat or cold, dryness or damp.
- Dust the wood and strings with a soft and clean cloth fairly and frequently.
- Replace strings before they show any signs of fraying and change them regularly for a brilliant tone. Always replace strings one by one and then re-tune (page 6).

Holding the guitar

Sit on a chair which has no arms and which is not so high that your feet cannot rest flat on the ground. Cross your right leg over your left and rest the guitar on your right thigh. Sit upright. The curve of your elbow, resting on the outer edge of the guitar body, should gently hold the guitar in position against your chest. Your left arm and hand are entirely free and do not support the guitar in any way.

What are notes?

Music is made up of sounds called notes: they range from very low sounds, to very high sounds. The notes are named by the first seven letters of the alphabet (A B C D E F G) which repeat over and over again, getting higher or lower.

Open strings

The strings of your guitar are each tuned to a different note. They must be tuned correctly before you can begin to play (see page 6). When you pluck a string and it vibrates, but your left-hand is not touching any frets on the neck, then it is said to be open. The lowest-sounding open string (the thickest one) is tuned to obtain the note E, therefore if you pluck it, the note you hear is E. The next string is tuned to obtain A, the next D, and so on in the order shown in the diagram below, until the thinnest string is tuned to high E.

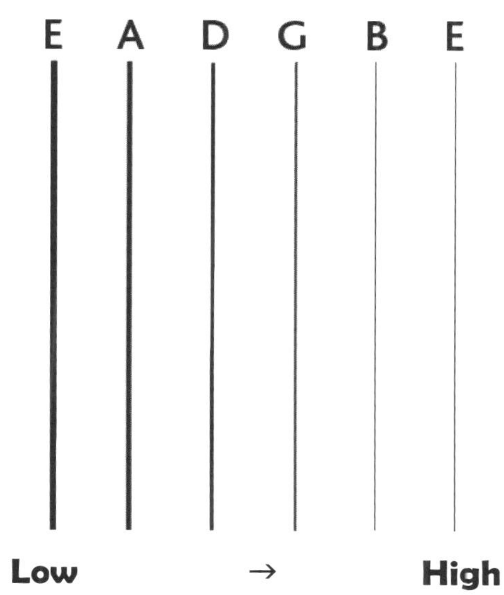

Tuning the guitar

The first track on the CDs are the tuning tracks. On it, you will hear clearly how each open string should sound when in tune. You must try to match your strings with these sounds, using the tuning pegs to adjust them.
If the string sounds lower than the note on the CD, you will need to tighten the string by turning the tuning peg, and If the string sounds higher you will need to slacken it.
Tuning can be tricky at first but it will become easier with practice and as your 'ear' begins to recognise the notes.

Tuning by fretting

Fretting is when your left-hand fingers press on the neck inside one or more of the frets. When you pluck or strum the string, it will create a note. If you are asked to fret the left hand on the E string, with finger three, in the third fret, you must count the frets from the top of the neck, and then press your third finger onto the correct string. When you pluck the string with your right hand, you will notice that it is a different sound than the open strings.

Tune only one string (low E - the thickest string) using the tuning track.
Next press down the low E string just behind the fifth fret (with your left-hand index finger). When plucked it will sound the note A - which should match the next open string.
Having tuned the A string, press down behind the fifth fret and it will sound the note D, which should match the next open string. Do the same again to obtain the correct pitch for the G string. To obtain the note B for the next string, press behind the **fourth fret**. Finally press the B string behind the fifth fret to obtain the note E – the last note that you need.

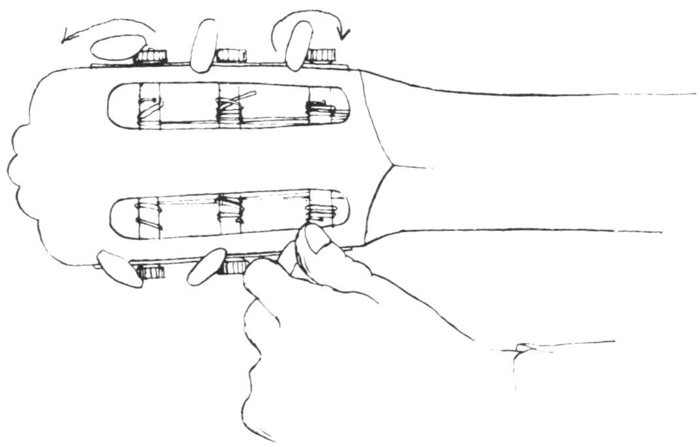

How to play notes

Rest the ball of your right-hand thumb on the E string where it passes over the sound-hole. Now sound the string with a firm downward stroke of the thumb, bringing it to rest against the next string (A). Keep the thumb straight and your wrist relaxed, and you can rest your fingertips on the other strings to steady your hand.
Practise playing all six open strings like this. You may also wish to pluck with a plectrum.

Left hand position

The diagram on this page indicates which fingers the numbers refer to on the chord diagram.
When fretting notes with the left hand, place your thumb in the middle of the back of the neck and press the strings down with the very tips of your fingers. Only your thumb and finger-tips should touch the neck.

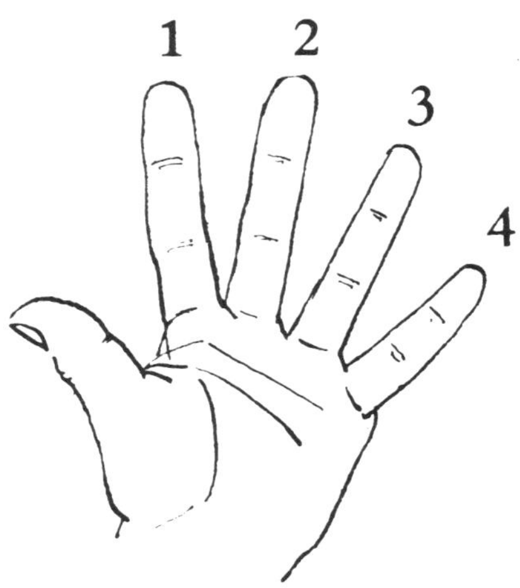

Chords

A chord is more than one note played at the same time. On the guitar, chords are played when the left hand frets and the right hand strums all, or some, of the strings.
Each chord has the same letter name as the bass note on which it is built – therefore the chord of A is built on the bass note of A. The bass note is sometimes called the root note as it is the root of the chord.
Below is the A major chord diagram. This shows where on the fingerboard to fret the strings in order to obtain the notes of an A major chord.

If you choose to accompany only with bass notes, as chords are too difficult to begin with, pluck only the highlighted (bold) string on the chord diagram (see below). Do not strum all strings unless you are playing the full chord. Sometimes the bass note is an open string (A major is an example of this). If the bass note is fretted, the highlighted string with have a circle with a finger number on it which you should fret with your left hand in the correct position.

The numbers in circles refer to the fingertips used to fret the strings.

The A major chord

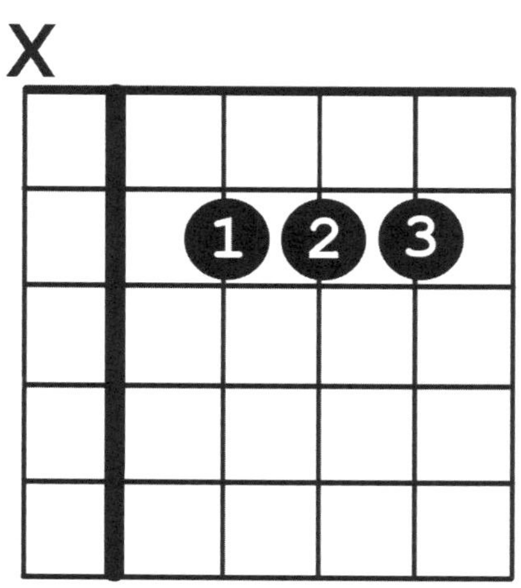

The chords to be played in an accompaniment are indicated by their letter names placed above the words of the song, like this **A**. A full index of chords can be found on pages 71 and 72.

If a note is muffled, it may be because you are pressing a string directly on top of a fret bar, or you may be touching a string which should be open.
If there are any buzzing sounds, you may not be pressing the strings firmly enough or closely enough to the fret.

When to strum

The songs in **Abracadabra Singalong Guitar** are in two-time, three-time and four-time. This means that you can clap in sets of two (1-2), three (1-2-3), or four (1-2-3-4) throughout the song. There is information regarding rhythm for each activity. Always listen and copy the guitar rhythms on the CD.
Aim to strum at least every time you see the chord letter above the lyrics. Listen to the tracks and copy what you hear. It is nice to create an accompanying rhythm, but do try the ones suggested here and keep them simple. There is more information on the downstrum and the upstrum on page 8.

Not all six strings are strummed with every chord. Do not brush the string with the X above it on the diagram.

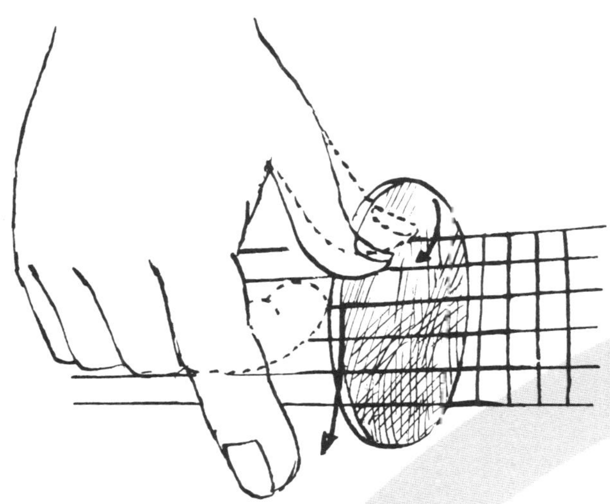

The A major chord

The D, G and B strings are all fretted to make the A major chord. In this book chords are represented as letters (eg, A) above the lyrics.
Look at the diagram below. Practise the shape of the chord, making sure that you use the correct fingertips in the left hand. Press your left hand fingers securely against the fret board to create a full, rich sound, neither too close nor too far away from the fret bars. Do not strum the string with the X above it when playing A (the E string). For an easier option just pluck the highlighted (bold) string in place of the chord. This is the root note of the chord, ,A and is an open string.

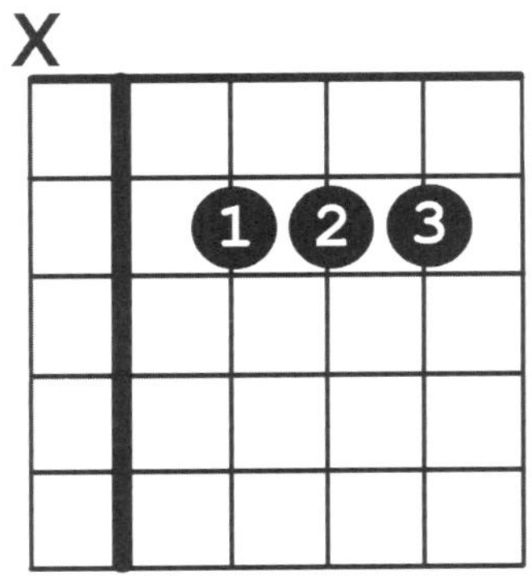

The E Major chord

Put the numbered fingers below on the strings. Copy the chord diagram below. The E Major chord has fretted notes on the A G and D strings using fingers 1, 2 and 3 of the left hand.
For an easier option just pluck the highlighted (bold) string in place of the chord. This is the root note of the chord, E, and is an open string.

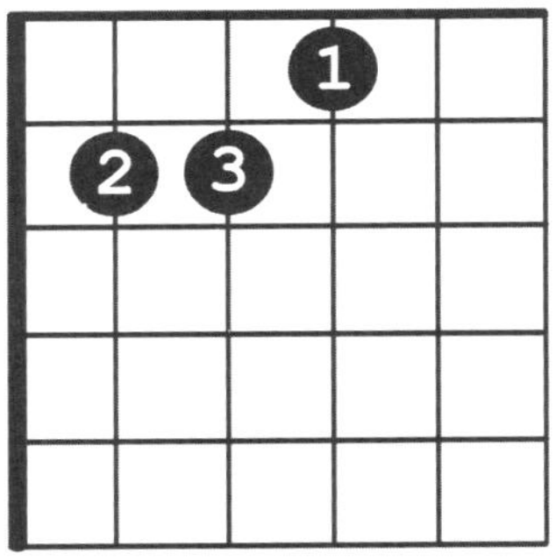

The down-strum

Press down the fretted strings firmly with fingertips indicated in the chord diagrams. Now, with the right-hand thumb held over the sound-hole, brush down across all the strings.

The up-strum

The sound of the up-strum is weaker than that of the down-strum so it is therefore usually played between strong beats rather than on them. For example, if the song is in four time (1-2-3-4), the up-strum will play on beats 2 and the 4.

1 Row, row, row your boat

2/3

Chords used in this song

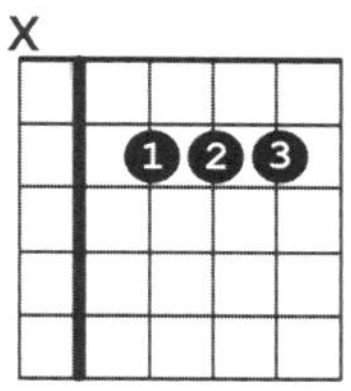

A major

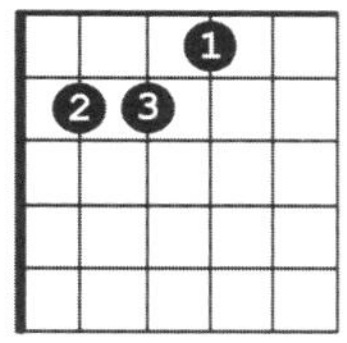

E major

A	A	A	A
Row,	**row,**	**row**	**your boat,**
A	A	A	A
Gently,	**down**	**the stream.**	
A	A	A	A
Merrily,	**merrily,**	**merrily,**	**merrily,**
E	E	A	A
Life	**is but**	**a dream.**	

Learn the song

Step 1

Learn the A chord. Strum the strings from top to bottom. Do exactly the same with the chord of E. Practise changing from one chord to the other and back again. If this is too difficult, pluck only the highlighted (bold) strings, instead of the chords to begin with.

Step 2

Listen to the performance track (02) and sing.
Clap as you sing. Count 1, 2, 3, 4; 1, 2, 3, 4 with the music.
Play the chords or bass notes, along to the music.
If you are playing chords,strum (dowstrum) once at the beginning of each line.

Step 3

Try strumming/plucking the guitar more often now. Rather than just one downstrum, try to strum twice or even four times per line, as above, incorporating an upstrum. This rhythm will match your clapping (step 2). When confident, sing and play with the backing track (03).

All together now

- **Sing as a round:** Divide the children into groups. Group 1 sings. When they reach the second line, group 2 starts the song. As you add more groups, they all begin one by one until everyone is singing a different part of the song at once. It takes concentration and practice. When confident, sing the round to the backing track (03).
- **Add guitarists and untuned percussion** (tambourines, drums, cymbals, maracas).

2 Ten in a bed

4/5

Chords used in this song

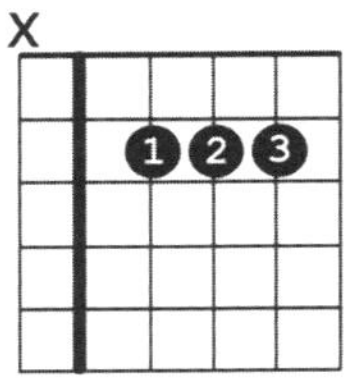

A major

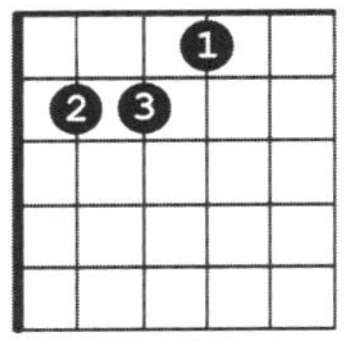

E major

A A A A
There were (ten) in a bed, and the little one said,
There was one in the bed, and the little one said,

A A A A
Roll over, roll over,
Good night (yawn).

A A A A
So they all rolled over and one fell out,

E E E E
Banged his head and gave a shout...

Learn the song

Step 1

Listen to the performance track (04). Most of the lyrics repeat, however the number 'in the bed' gets lower (line 1), and the last verse is different. Learn the structure of the song using the CD and be sure of the order before moving on to the guitar.
Revise chords A and E using pages 8 & 9. Pluck the highlighted strings (bass notes) in place of the chords to begin with if the chords are difficult.

Step 2

Play the chords or bass notes slowly without the CD. Sing along while you play if possible. Try to keep a constant speed (or *tempo* as it is known in music). Try not to slow down when you change chord/string.
Now play the CD. Clap to the music to get a natural feel for the rhythm that you will strum or pluck. Try to strum once per line at first.

Step 3

Listen to the backing track (05) and sing. Imagine/mime with your guitar when you will strum and the left-hand chord positions or bass notes.
Play in order with the backing track or without the CD.
The more advanced player can strum every time they see a chord letter above the lyrics - four per line.
Even more difficult is the guitar rhythm in verse 3.
Listen to the CD and copy.

All together now

- All listen to the performance track of *Ten in a bed* (04). **Divide the singers** into five or ten groups and decide which group sings which verse. Ensure that everyone clearly knows which number verse they are singing. Practise with the performance track (04) and then with the backing track (05) once confident.
- Choose a selection of the groups, or all groups to **play the guitar**. It might be too difficult to sing and play at once to begin with, in which case divide the class into 'singers' and 'players', with the 'singers' performing every verse. Remember that some players can strum only the bass note (highlighed open string on the chord diagrams) if they prefer.
- Give some singers **untuned percussion instruments** so that they can tap, shake or beat in time to the music. Urge them to create their own simple rhythms that suit the music. Another idea is for the singers to clap in time.

3 He's got the whole world in his hands

6/7

Chords used in this song

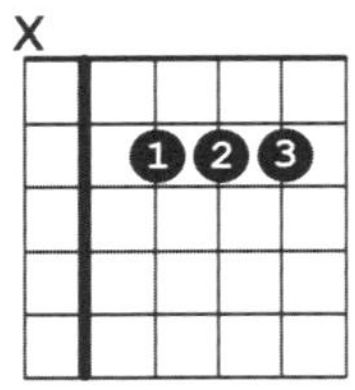

A major

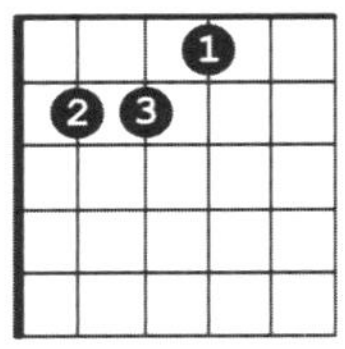

E major

	A	A	A	A
1. He's got the	**whole**	**world**	**in his**	**hands,**
2. He's got the	**sun and the**	**rain**	**in his**	**hands,**
3. He's got the	**moon and the**	**stars**	**in his**	**hands,**
4. He's got the	**wind and the**	**clouds**	**in his**	**hands,**
5. He's got the	**rivers and the**	**mountains**	**in his**	**hands,**
6. He's got	**everybody**	**here**	**in his**	**hands.**

	E	E	E	E
1. He's got the	**whole**	**world**	**in his**	**hands,**
2. He's got the	**sun and the**	**rain**	**in his**	**hands,**
3. He's got the	**moon and the**	**stars**	**in his**	**hands,**
4. He's got the	**wind and the**	**clouds**	**in his**	**hands,**
5. He's got the	**rivers and the**	**mountains**	**in his**	**hands,**
6. He's got	**everybody**	**here**	**in his**	**hands.**

	A	A	A	A
1. He's got the	**whole**	**world**	**in his**	**hands,**
2. He's got the	**sun and the**	**rain**	**in his**	**hands,**
3. He's got the	**moon and the**	**stars**	**in his**	**hands,**
4. He's got the	**wind and the**	**clouds**	**in his**	**hands,**
5. He's got the	**rivers and the**	**mountains**	**in his**	**hands,**
6. He's got	**everybody**	**here**	**in his**	**hands.**

	E	E	A	A
1. He's got the	**whole world**	**in his**	**hands.**	
2. He's got the	**whole world**	**in his**	**hands.**	
3. He's got the	**whole world**	**in his**	**hands.**	
4. He's got the	**whole world**	**in his**	**hands.**	
5. He's got the	**whole world**	**in his**	**hands.**	
6. He's got the	**whole world**	**in his**	**hands.**	

Learn the song

Step 1

Listen to the CD and sing along. Make sure that you are happy with the structure and how to follow the lyric sheet (the verses are numbered). Try to hear when the guitar is playing. This song uses chords A and E again. If at any point you feel that strumming the whole chord is too difficult, just pluck the highlighted (bold) string (see chord diagram). Do not touch the other strings or fret with your left hand.

Step 2

Practise the change between A major and E major. The last change of each verse is fast so practise slowly before you try to play at the same speed (*tempo*) as the CD.
Try to play the whole song and sing without the CD.

Step 3

Play with the performance track (06). Strum every time you see a chord letter above the lyrics - four per line. Follow the lyric page but notice that the strumming does not start until the word 'whole.' Try to strum more often if possible, taking inspiration from the guitarist on the CD.

All together now

- Some members of the group can **play the guitar** while others can **sing and play percussion instruments**. Choose a selection of untuned percussion instruments, such as drums, tambourines and woodblocks.

Create simple rhythms together: Tambourine players might play:

He's got the whole world in his hands,

And the woodblocks might play:

He's got the whole world in his hands,

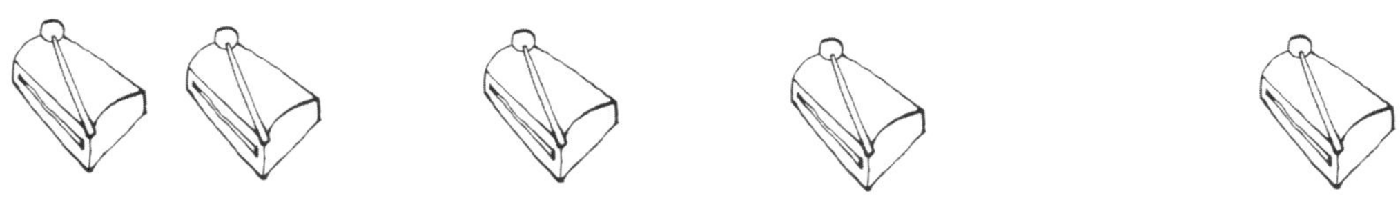

- Ask the singers to **create movements** to demonstrate the lyrics, eg, they might make the shape of the world for the first verse with their hands, or wriggle their fingers to represent the rain.
- On the last verse – 'everybody here' – you can hear a clapped rhythm on the CD. Choose some of the group to learn the rhythm and teach everybody else.

The G major chord

This is quite a difficult chord to stretch and requires practice before you attempt to play a song in which it is in. Look at the chord diagram below.
Practise changing from G major to D major and back again several times until you are comfortable enough to start learning songs with the chord in. If it is too difficult to play the chord, it is easier to first play the bass note. To do this, play the highlighted (bold) string on the diagram but make sure that your second finger is pressed firmly on the third fret (as shown).

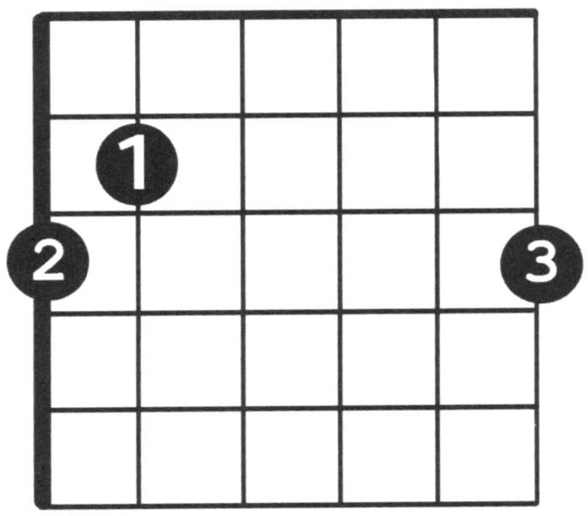

The D major chord

The D chord is fretted on the three highest strings - the G, B and high E strings. Practise the chord, copy the shape below and make sure that you use the correct fingers. Notice that it makes a triangular shape on the fret board.
When you play the D chord do not strum all the strings. Do not strum the first two strings (low E and A) but instead strum the D open string and the three strings that are fretted. If playing the chord is too difficult to begin with, play only the bass note. To do this, pluck the highlighted (bold) string on the chord diagram below. It is an open string so your left hand does not press against the fret board.

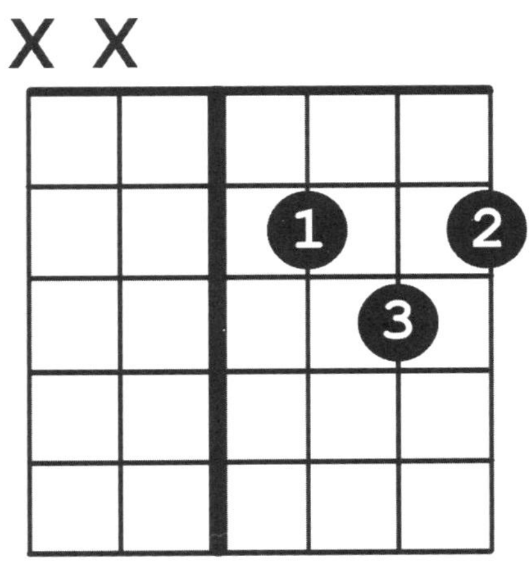

4 London's burning

Chords used in this song

8/9

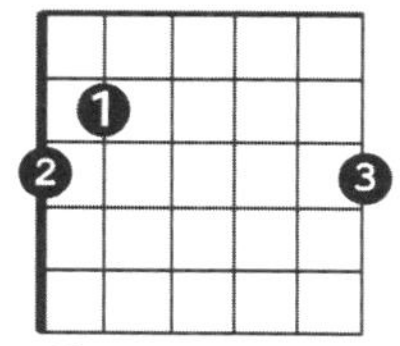

G major

G	G		G	G
London's	burn -	ing,	London's	burn -	ing

	G	G		G	G
London's	burn -	ing,	London's	burn -	ing
Fetch the	eng -	ines,	fetch the	eng -	ines
Fire	fire,		fire	fire?	
Pour on	wa -	ter,	pour on	wa -	ter.

Learn the song

Step 1

Read page 14 and learn the G major chord or bass note.
It is difficult to stretch. If you cannot manage it to begin with, only play the highlighted string on the chord diagram.
This time the bass note needs to be fretted with finger '2' (see diagram and pg, 14).

Step 2

Try to play the song and sing without the CD.
Strum the chords when you see the chord letter above the lyrics. The chords only play on beats 2 & 3.

1	2	3
Wait	strum	strum

Step 3

Play the song with the CD tracks. At first do not sing, only strum. Then, either sing by yourself, or have someone else sing along to the well-known tune while you play.
Only use the downstrum for this song.

All together now

- **Sing as a round** with or without the backing track. An explanation of a round can be found on page 11 (*Ten in a bed*).
- Give the singers **untuned percussion instruments** (tambourines, woodblocks and bongos), or create a separate group of percussionists. They can keep a regular beat. Listen to the backing track and copy the guitar rhythms that you hear before creating original rhythms.
- Some can **play an ostinato** on xylophones, glockenspiels or keyboards. An ostinato is a repeated pattern of notes. Choose people to play it over and over again all through the piece. They can practise first with the CD. It matches exactly the rhythm for 'London's burning'.

Lon -	don's	burn	-	ing
D	D	G		G

5 Silent night

10/11

Chords used in this song

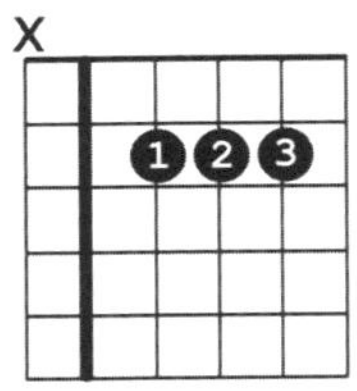

A major

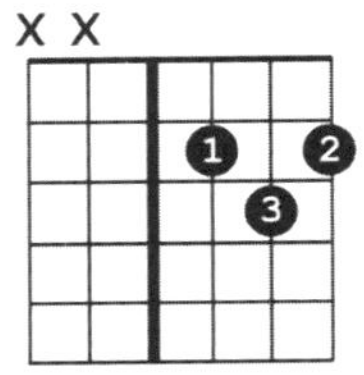

D major

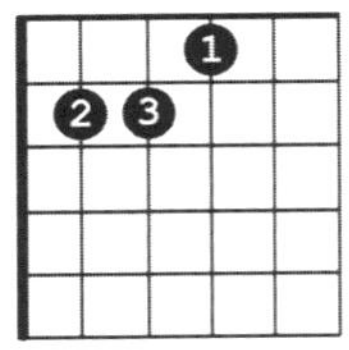

E major

	A	A	A	A
1.	Silent	night,	holy	night,
2.	Silent	night,	holy	night,
3.	Silent	night,	holy	night,
	E	**E**	**A**	**A**
1.	All is	calm,	all is	bright,
2.	Shepherds	quake	at the	sight,
3.	Son of	God,	love's pure	light,
	D	**D**	**A**	**A**
1.	Round yon	Vir - gin	Mother and	Child,
2.	Glories	stream from	heaven a -	far,
3.	Radiant	beams from	Thy holy	face,
	D	**D**	**A**	**A**
1.	Holy	Infant so	tender and	mild,
2.	Heavenly	hosts sing	Allelu -	ia,
3.	With the	dawn of	redeeming	grace,
	E	**E**	**A**	**A**
1.	Sleep in	heavenly	pea -	ce,
2.	Christ, the	Saviour is	bo -	rn,
3.	Jesus,	Lord, at Thy	bir -	th,
	A	**E**	**A**	**A**
1.	Sleep in	heavenly	peace.	
2.	Christ, the	Saviour is	born.	
3.	Jesus,	Lord, at Thy	birth.	

Learn the song

Step 1

Silent night introduces songs with three chords. A major and E major have been played before. Read page 14 to learn D major. Thankfully it is slow, allowing time to change chord. Practise the chords again, referring to the instruction pages if need be (pgs. 8 and 14). Other Christmas songs in *Abracadabra Singalong Guitar* are *Away in a manger* (pg, 24) and *Jingle bells* (pg, 46).

Step 2

Play the chords very slowly at first (without the CD) and then increase the speed as you become more confident. If this is too hard, first master just plucking one open string in place of each chord (the highlighted, bold string on the chord diagram) rather than strumming the entire chord.

Step 3

Now try playing the chords, first without the music and then with the performance track (10).
Strum once per chord, then more often, until you strum at least every time you see a chord letter above the lyrics. Listen to tracks 10 and 11 to hear effective guitar rhythms. Try to copy what you hear. Sing as you play along to the backing track (11). If you need to, try this song at a much slower speed, simply turn off the CD and play.

All together now

- *Silent night* is a simple, beautiful Christmas carol, and the backing does not need anything too complicated. Give as many of the group as possible a guitar and, after listening to the CD tracks more than once, allow them to **strum slowly in time to the music**. First all play together with the performance track (10).
- Once everyone in the group is happy with the guitar part, ensure that everyone can see the lyric page (pg, 16), You can photocopy it or project it. **Sing the carol** all the way through with or without the CD.
- **All sing and play the guitar** along to the backing track. Perform the song without the CD.
- Give some individuals an untuned percussion instrument, eg, bells, maracas or a tambourine, instead of a guitar. They can **create an original rhythm** to accompany the song. Listen to the backing track for ideas.

C major

This is a fairly difficult chord to stretch. Practise changing from C major to many of the other chords that you have learnt so far. Do not strum the low E string (the string with the X above it on the diagram). If playing the chord is too difficult, simply play the highlighted (bold) string with the third left-hand finger fretted as shown. This is the bass note of the chord C major.

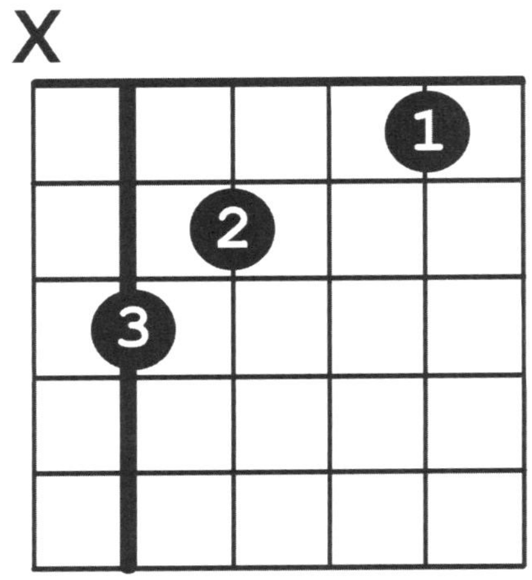

Minor chords - Am and Em

Here for the first time in the book you need to play a minor chord. Up until this point they have been major chords, which we have simply called by their letter names.
Minor chords are made up of a slightly different combination of notes from their major counterparts and the result is a rather more sad sound. They are distinguished from major chords by the small letter 'm' written after the letter name of the chord.
The chords here are A minor and E minor. Practise the shapes below. The A minor chord is the same shape as the E major chord but in a different place on the fretboard. E minor is the A minor chord, but without finger 1 (see below). To only play the bass notes, pluck the highlighted (bold) strings on the diagram. They are both open chords. Do not strum the E string when playing A minor (the string with the X above it).

Am

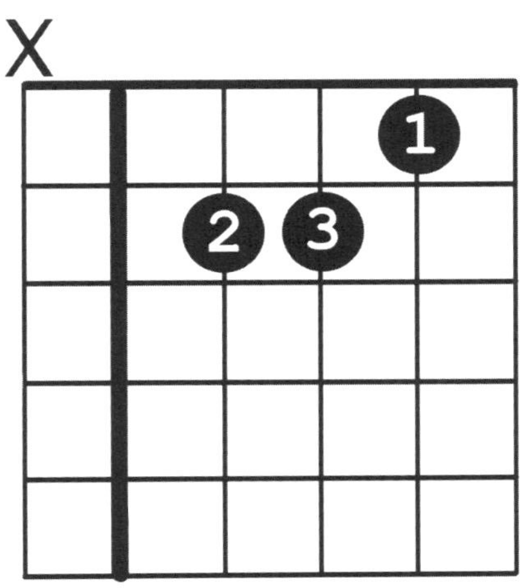

Em

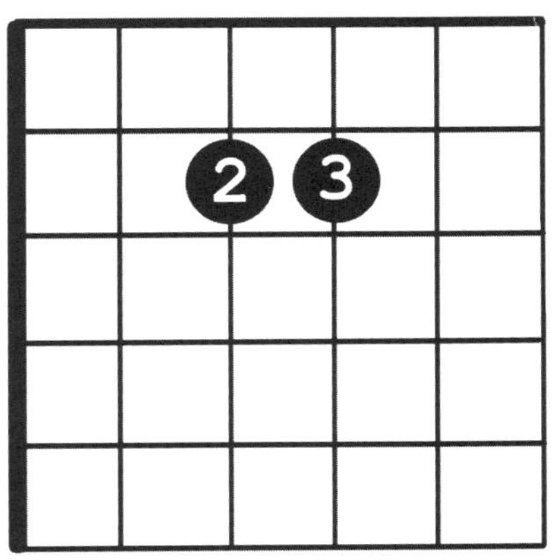

6 Frere Jacques

12/13

Chords used in this song

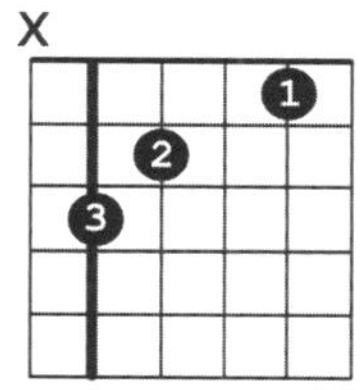

C major

C	C	C	C
Frere	**Jacques,**	**Frere**	**Jacques,**
C	C	C	C
Dormez	**- vous?**	**Dormez -**	**vous?**
C	C	C	C
Sonnez les	**matines,**	**sonnez les**	**matines,**
C	C	C	C
Ding dang	**dong,**	**ding dang**	**dong.**

Learn the song

Step 1

This song has one chord, but it is a new chord. Practise playing C Major many times before you begin (see pg, 18). An easier option is to only play the highlighted (bold) string on the chord diagram with finger '3' fretted as shown. Try to move on to play the full chord.

Step 2

Listen to the CD. At first the guitar does not strum very often, however it builds until different more interesting rhythms are played.
Try to copy the strumming rhythms on the CD.
If this is too difficult just downstrum when you see the chord letter above the lyric - four times per line.

Step 3

Make up your own strumming rhythms. Try playing them without the CD, therefore, deciding which rhythms sound best before accompanying the track. Finally sing while you play to either the backing track (13) or alone.

All together now

- **Sing as a round** with or without the backing track (explanation of a round, pg 11).
- Some or all can **play the guitar chords/bass notes** with the singers.
  Give a few of the group tuned percussion instruments. The following ostinati can be played repeatedly throughout the song. Let the player decide which one they prefer.

Fre	**-re**	**Jacques**
C	G	C

Fre	**-re**	**Jacques**
E	C	E

7 She'll be coming round the mountain

14/15

Chords used in this song

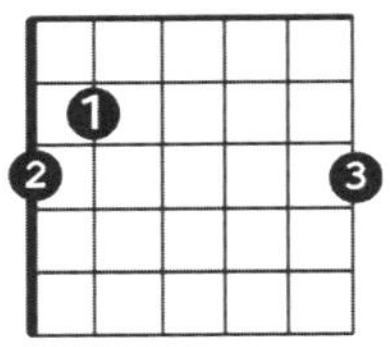

G major

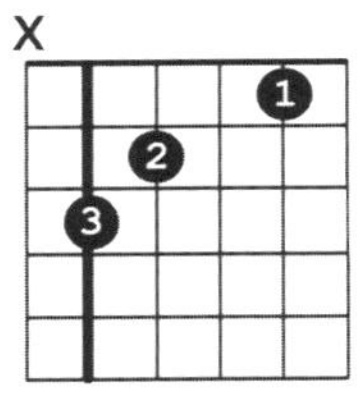

C major

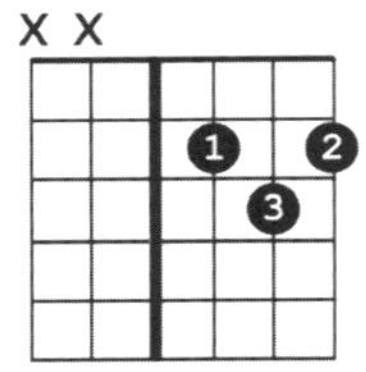

D major

VERSE 1

G G

1. She'll be coming round the mountain when she comes,

G D

1. She'll be coming round the mountain when she comes,

G C C

1. She'll be coming round the mountain, coming round the mountain,

G D G

1. Coming round the mountain when she comes.

VERSE 2

2. She'll be driving six white horses when she comes...

3. Oh we'll all come out to meet her when she comes...

4. She'll be wearing red pajamas when she comes...

5. We'll be singing Alleluia when she comes...

CHORUS (sung after verses 2,3 & 4)

G G G D

Singing aye aye yippie yippie aye. Singing aye aye yippie yippie aye.

G C G D G

Singing aye aye yippie aye aye yippie, aye aye yippie yippie aye.

Learn the song

Step 1

Revise the chords. The change, G D G for the last line of the chorus and verse, is fairly fast and will need practice. If you are in any doubt about when to play and change chords, listen to the backing track (15). In the first verse you can clearly hear the strum of the guitar. It is slow and quite infrequent, meaning that it is easy to shape your fingers in time for the next chord. Play only the highlighted bass notes otherwise (see chord diagrams).

Step 2

Listen to the tracks. In verse two the strumming becomes more frequent. Try to play along to the backing track (15).
Notice that the strumming rhythm changes with every verse. They become harder as the song progresses. Verse 3 has lots of strumming, while verse 4 strums on the offbeat. If you count 1-2-3-4 along to the music, the offbeat strum would be on the 2 and the 4, rather than the stronger 1 and 3.

Step 3

Without the CD play and sing the song at a slow pace. When you feel comfortable with the chord changes and lyrics, perform to the backing track (15). Use the performamce track to confirm the lyrics and structure of the song.

All together now

- By nature this is an upbeat 'rip-roaring' country sing-along so works brilliantly for group performances. For the best effect, everyone in the group should **sing.** Try splitting the singers so that different people sing each verse and everyone joins in for the chorus.
- Then **add the instruments**. Some or all of the group can play the guitar along to the performance track (14). It is possible to just play the bass notes (represented by the highlighted strings on the diagrams) instead of strumming the full chord. Remember to pluck only this note rather than brush all the strings and fret if required (G major and C major).
- **Add percussion to the performance**. 'Clip clop' percussive sounds with coconut shells or woodblocks can be used to represent the horse. Also add some 'yee ha's!' in a cowboy style. Play other country music to the group and ask them for ideas to enhance the performance. Play with the backing track (14) and finally aim for a live performance with no CD at all.
- **Add some barn dancing** or create a role-play 'cowboy' area in the classroom. Learn some simple barn dance moves and teach the group. This would work fantastically well for an assembly or choir performance.

8 What will we do with the drunken sailor?

16/17

Chords used in this song

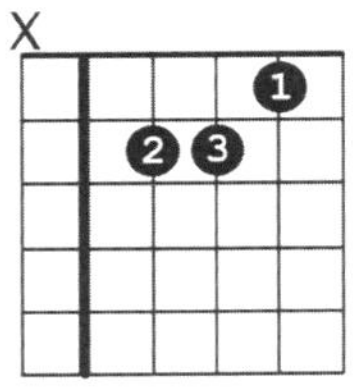

A minor

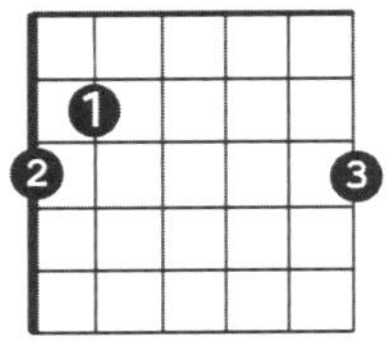

G major

VERSES

Am Am
1. What will we do with the drunken sailor?

G G
1. What will we do with the drunken sailor?

Am Am
1. What will we do with the drunken sailor?

G Am
1-6 Earl-aye in the mor - ning.

CHORUS (sung after every verse, except the last)

Am
Hoo-ray and up she rises,
G
Hoo-ray and up she rises,
Am
Hoo-ray and up she rises,
G Am
Earl-aye in the morning.

OTHER VERSES

2. Take 'im and shake 'im and try an' wake 'im...
3. Give 'im a dose of soap and water...
4. Shave his belly with a rusty razor...
5. Put him in the guard room till he's sober...
6. That's what we'll do with the drunken sailor...

Learn the song

Step 1

Listen to the backing track (17) first. Don't be put off by how fast the song sounds, as the chords strum slowly. Listen for the guitar.
Revise the Aminor chord and the G major chord. Try to change as fluently as possible.
Listen to the performance track (16) now and mime or play in time to the music.
Only strum each chord once to begin with or play only the bass notes.

Step 2

Find the natural pulse of the music by clapping or counting in time to the performance track (16).
Work towards four strums per line (strum at least every time you see a chord letter above the lyrics).

The last verse does not have a break, but leads straight into the last verse.

Step 3

Without the CD try to play verse 1 all the way through, with fluent changes between the two chords. Have the lyrics in front of you and sing as you play. Work out a number of strums per chord or a strumming rhythm that you like and can manage. Use both the downstrum and the upstrum and take inspiration from, or copy, what is played on the CD.

All together now

- First make sure that everyone can see a copy of the lyrics sheet. Once everyone is happy with the lyrics ask some or all to **try singing the song** with a fun, sailor/pirate accent (listen to track 16). Dress up as sailors and pirates and urge the children to get into character with 'ahoy there matey' and 'oohh aah!'. Make sure that everyone is certain of the order of verses and choruses.
- As you **sing, clap or stamp your feet in time to the music**. It will suit the raucous characters for the performance too.
- Some of the group can sing while the others **play the guitar, clap, or experiment with which untuned percussion instruments suits the accompaniment best**. Tambourines and drums playing a steady pulse will work well.
- You can **divide the vocal into two parts** - question and answer phrases. One half can sing the question verses ('What will we do with the drunken sailor?') and then the other half can answer them - 'take 'im and shake 'im.'
- Choose some children to try whistling along to the music (as on the CD track).

9 Away in a manger

18/19

Chords used in this song

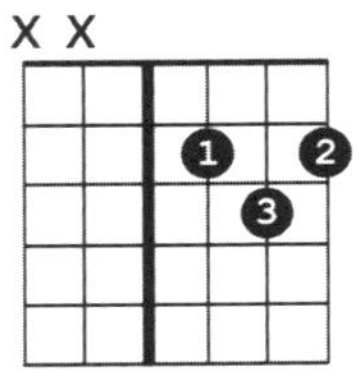

D major

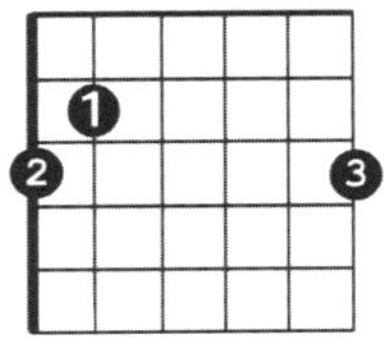

G major

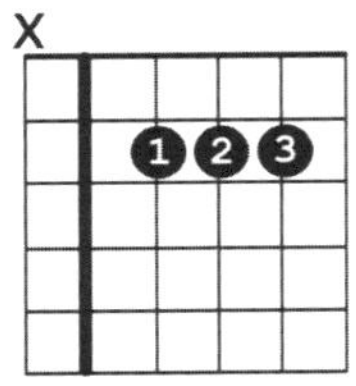

A major

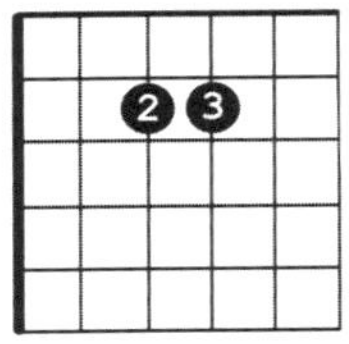

E minor

D — G

1. A- way in a manger, no crib for a bed,
2. The cattle are lowing, the poor baby wakes,
3. Be near me, Lord Jesus, I ask thee to stay,

G — D — Em — A

1. The little Lord Jesus, laid down his sweet head.
2. But little Lord Jesus, no cry he makes.
3. Close by me for- ever, and love me I pray.

D — G

1. The stars in the bright sky, looked down where he lay,
2. I love thee, Lord Jesus, Look down from the sky,
3. Bless all the dear children, in thy tender care,

G — D — A — D

1. The little Lord Jesus, a-sleep on the hay.
2. And stay by my side, 'til morn -ing is nigh.
3. And take us to heaven, to live with thee there.

Learn the song

Step 1

Away in a manger uses one new chord, E Minor. Read page 18 and learn the chord, using the chord diagram. Play the new chord as many times as you need to until you can play it confidently. Listen to both tracks (18 & 19). Play only the bass notes if you need to (these are the highlighted strings on the chord diagrams).

Step 2

Look at the lyrics and the chords on page 24. Without the CD, try to slowly play through the chords. You do not have to sing along or even strum each chord more than once. Instead, concentrate on changing the chords fluently. Without the CD, try singing as you play. Start with verse 1 only and then attempt more.

Step 3

Listen to track 18. Notice that you must first wait for the introduction to finish before playing. Listen out for the guitar chords. which play quite slowly. There is no need to strum more often, as this rhythm suits the song.
Play to the backing track (19) or sing and play the song without the CD. Copy the guitar rhythm that you hear on the CD.

All together now

- A Christmas classic, *Away in a manger* is a favourite for group singing and classes, particularly for Christmas concerts and assemblies.
- First, **ensure that everyone is familiar with, and has a copy of, the lyrics (pg, 24)**. Go slowly through any lines or old-fashioned words that the group may not be familiar with. Tell the group the nativity story. Ask them to point out individual words or lines that they have not heard before, eg, 'crib', 'ye', 'thy', and discover their meaning together.
- Listen to the performance track and **sing along, verse-by-verse with the recording**.
- Now a group, or the leader, can **play the guitar while the others sing**. The guitarist/s can practise the guitar part alone, while the singers learn the lyrics. When everyone is together, give a selection of singers bells or triangles to play during the song, to add to the 'Christmassy' sound. They should decide between themselves when and what they will play, otherwise the accompaniment will become too confused. Use the CD for inspiration.
- **Perform the song** with the backing track (19) or live, with instruments and no CD. For assemblies or concerts the group can dress up as characters from the nativity story and act out a scene before playing the song.

10 Wild thing

20/21

Chords used in this song

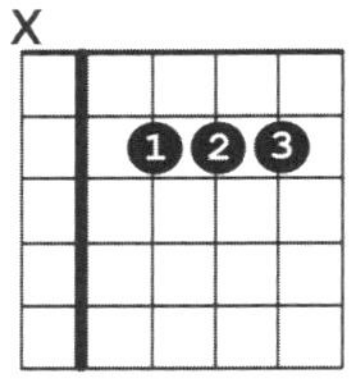

A major

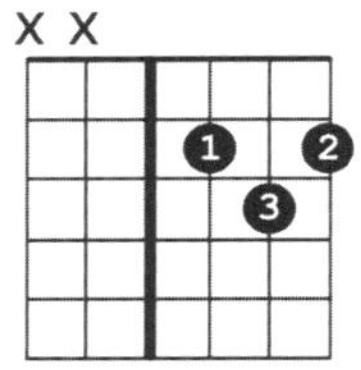

D major

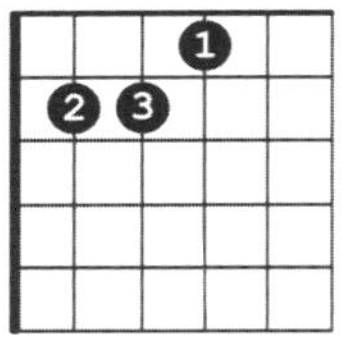

E major

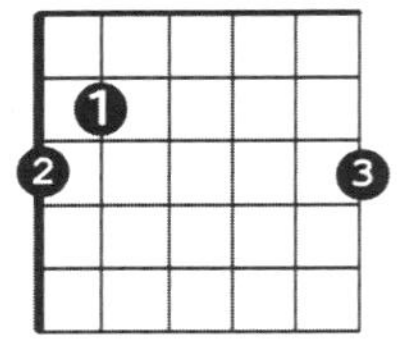

G major

A A DDEED D A A DD EE D D
Wild thing... you make my heart sing... you make

A A DD EE DD A A DD E EEE
everything, groovy... wild thing...

GAGA **Wild thing, I think I love you,**
GAGA **But I wanna know for sure,**
GAGA **Come on, hold me tight...**
GAGA **I love you.**

A A DDEED D A A DD EE D D
Wild thing... you make my heart sing... you make

A A DD EE DD A A DD E EEE
everything, groovy... wild thing...

GAGA **Wild thing, I think you move me,**
GAGA **But I wanna know for sure,**
GAGA **So come on, hold me tight...**
GAGA **You move me.**

REPEAT VERSE AND INSTRUMENTAL

Learn the song

Step 1

Do you know this rock classic? Listen to the performance track (20) and find the original version performed by a band called The Troggs.
Although the chords are written above the lyrics, it is important that you listen to the track many times to learn the guitar rhythm. Play only the highlighted strings/bass notes on the diagrams if you find the chords too difficult.

Step 2

Now put down your guitar and sing along to the performance track (20) and then the backing track (21). Learn where the voice appears and disappears in the middle part of the song.

Step 3

Play to the backing track (21). Do not sing the lyrics or melody line but try to stay in time with the chord changes. If this is too challenging at first, turn the CD off and practise slowly until you can match the speed of the CD.
Try singing and playing the guitar at the same time. If you have access to an electric guitar, try playing the chords on it and be impressed with the sound that you make.

All together now

- This is a very well-known rock song and a fun, different choice for a group performance. **Make sure that the group sing it with lots of energy and 'attitude,'** particularly for the spoken parts. It might be quite nice to choose individual/duet singers to perform the spoken parts, eg, 'Wild thing, I think I love you.'
- If anyone can play the drums or bass try to **create a rock band** to accompany the singers and join the guitarists. If not, give some of the singers a drum and sticks to play. Make sure that they decide on a rhythm beforehand and all play the same thing, otherwise the rhythms will sound untidy.
- Listen to the track again. You will notice that during the middle of the song when there is a **percussion break** played by a woodblock and a maraca. Choose some members of the group to learn and replicate this percussion part on the same or different instruments.
- There is a **guitar solo** in this piece. It is difficult to learn at first although with practice competent musicians could try working it out by trial and error using their 'ear' – the mark of a great rock musician! In the meantime some singers might 'la, la, la' this part as a second vocal line, and carry it on over into the rest of the song. Experiment with where this second vocal part fits successfully in the accompaniment.

11 Little brown jug

22/23

Chords used in this song

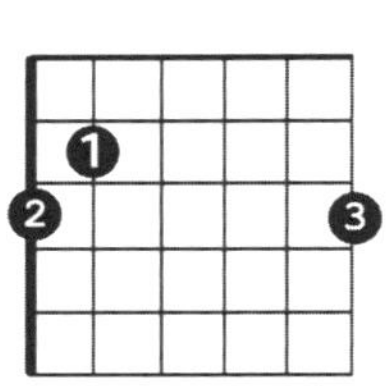

G major

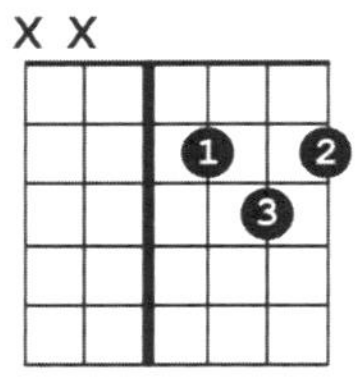

D major

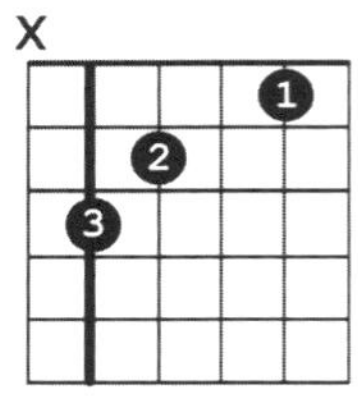

C major

Verse 1

G C D G
My wife and I live all alone, In a wee log hut we call our own.

G C D G
I/she like gin and I/she likes rum, And my don't we have lots of fun.

Chorus:

G C D G
Ha ha ha, hee hee hee, Little brown jug don't I love thee?

G C D G
Ha ha ha, hee hee hee, Little brown jug don't I love thee.

Verse 2

G C D G
When I go toiling on the farm I take the jug under my arm;

G C D G
I place it under a shady tree, Little brown jug, just you and me.

Chorus

Verse 3

G C D G
Bought a cow from Farmer Jones, And she was nothing but skin and bones,

G C D G
I fed her up as fine as silk, She jumped a fence and strained her milk.

Chorus

Repeat verse 1

Chorus

Learn the song

Step 1

The chords in this song have already been learnt. Take the time to go over each of the chords, D major, G major & C major, until you have memorised them. *Little brown jug* has some fast changes, so know the chords before you attempt the whole song. Particularly practise changing from one chord to another.

Step 2

Listen to the performance track (22) and learn the song. Sing it without the guitar first. Next, strum the chords to the performance track (22) or without the CD. Strum each chord once to begin with. It is easier to play only the highlighted bass notes/strings (see bold strings on chord diagrams).

Step 3

Play the chords with the backing track (23). Work up to playing and singing at the same time, still only strumming very slowly. You will notice on the backing/performance track that the guitar is very simple for the verse while in the chorus, it has a more complex rhythm. When confident, copy the rhythm on the CD.

All together now

- Listen to *Little brown Jug* together as a group. Make sure that everyong can see the lyrics and sing the whole song. Notice that the chorus and verse 1 are repeated except for a change in line two. **Sing with the CD** until the group is confident about the lyrics and structure. All **clap a natural pulse to the song**. Divide the group into four. Each group sings one verse and everyone joins in at the chorus. Alternate the 'ha ha ha' and the 'hee hee hee' between the groups.
- **Give a few members of each group a guitar**, or one person can lead the whole group. Those without guitars sing and clap as before. The guitarist/s should aim to strum in time with the clapping.
- Replace the clapping with **untuned percussion instruments**. Ask the percussionists to create different, interesting rhythms with their instruments.

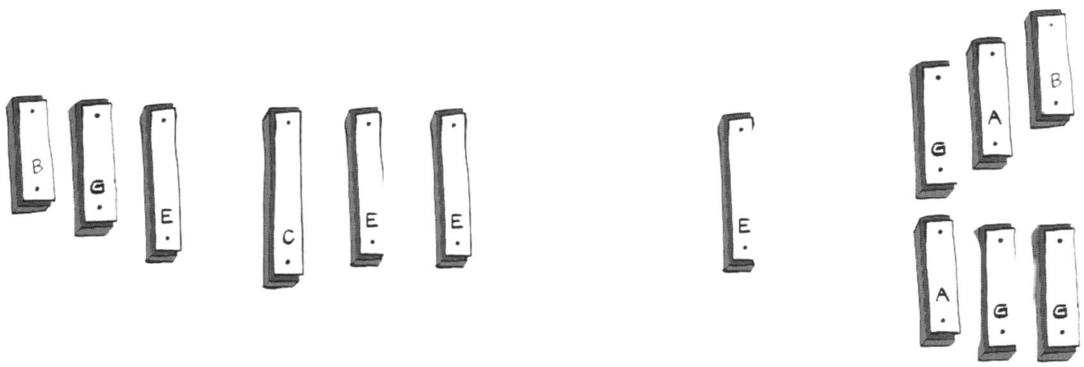

- Some of the group can **play the melody line on tuned percussion** (with the chorus only or throughout - see above). The xylophone, chime bars, glockenspiel, or even a keyboard suit this part.

12 Rock around the clock

24/25

Chords used in this song

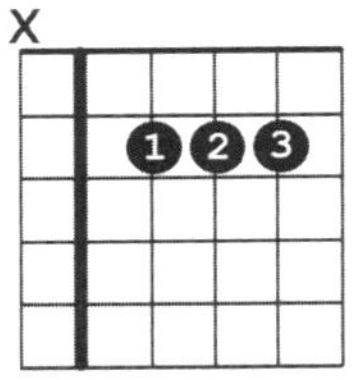

A major

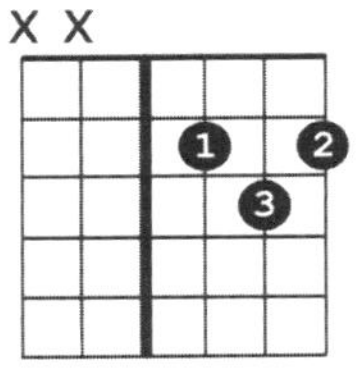

D major

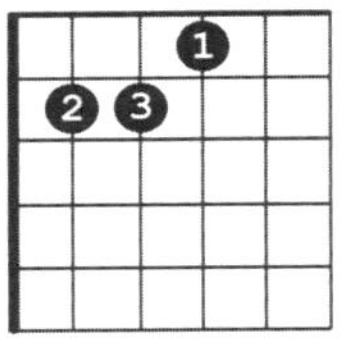

E major

A (at the beginning of each of the first three lines)
One, two, three o'clock, four o'clock, rock,
Five, six, seven o'clock, eight o'clock, rock,
Nine, ten, eleven o'clock, twelve o'clock, rock,

E
We're gonna rock around the clock tonight.

A
Put your glad rags on, and join me, hon,

A
We'll have some fun when the clock strikes one,

CHORUS

D
We're gonna rock around the clock tonight,

A
We're gonna rock, rock, rock, 'til broad daylight.

E A
We're gonna rock, gonna rock, around the clock tonight.

A
When the clock strikes two, three and four,

A
If the band slows down we'll yell for more,

CHORUS

A
When the chimes ring five, six and seven,

A
We'll be right in seventh heaven.

CHORUS and INSTRUMENTAL

A

When it's eight, nine, ten, eleven too,

A

I'll be goin' strong and so will you.

CHORUS

A

When the clock strikes twelve, we'll cool off then,
Start a-rockin' round the clock again.

CHORUS

Learn the song

Step 1

Listen to the performance track. *Rock around the clock* is a classic rock and roll song by Bill Haley and the comets. Try to find and listen to the original and other rock and roll songs. Sing along to the performance track (24). Learn the lyrics and structure using pages 30 and 31.

Step 2

Revise the chords. Practise the chords in the correct order without the CD or vocals. The chord letters are above the lyrics. Strum the chords as many times as you like before changing. Listen to the guitar on the CD and copy: It plays much slower than you think! An easier option is to play the open strings in place of the chords (see bold strings on chord diagrams, pg, 30).

Step 3

Sing and play first to the track with the vocal (24) and then to the backing track only (25). As the song moves along, the guitarist strums more frequently – try this. The song is in four time (you can count/clap 1-2-3-4 along to the music). Strum on 1-2-3-4 or more, using the downstrum and upstrum.

All together now

- This is enormous fun to **perform as a group**. Split the group and give them each a verse to learn and sing (everyone can sing/speak the introduction). Everyone must learn the chorus, as everyone will sing the chorus together.
- Choose another group to **play the guitar**. Up to five people only should play the guitar at once. Swap the guitarists around so that everyone gets a chance to play.
- **Introduce drums** to keep a steady beat so that everyone stays in time. Anyone who plays the piano can try to play the chords or bass notes.
- Some children can have guitars but **only play the bass notes**. These are the highlighted open strings in the chord diagrams (page 30).
- Show the group some rock and roll costumes and dancing. For a performance, some could **perform some rock and roll dancing** and everyone can dress up in authentic 1950's clothes.

13 The animals went in two by two

2/3

Chords used in this song

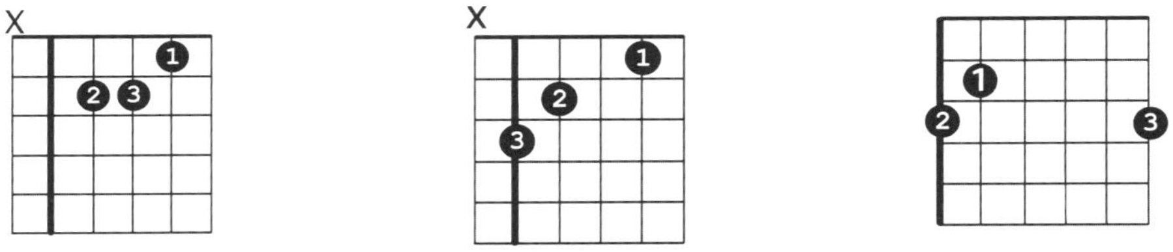

A minor C major G major

Am C

1. The animals went in two by two, hurrah! hurrah!
2. The animals went in three by three, hurrah! hurrah!
3. The animals went in four by four, hurrah! hurrah!
4. The animals went in five by five, hurrah! hurrah!
5. The animals went in six by six, hurrah! hurrah!
6. The animals went in seven by seven, hurrah! hurrah!

Am C E

1. The animals went in two by two, hurrah! hurrah!
2. The animals went in three by three, hurrah! hurrah!
3. The animals went in four by four, hurrah! hurrah!
4. The animals went in five by five, hurrah! hurrah!
5. The animals went in six by six, hurrah! hurrah!
6. The animals went in seven by seven, hurrah! hurrah!

Am G C E

1. The animals went in two by two, the elephant and the kangaroo...
2. The animals went in three by three, the wasp, the ant and the bumble bee...
3. The animals went in four by four,the great hippopotamus stuck in the door...
4. The animals went in five by five they warmed each other to keep alive...
5. The animals went in six by six they turned out the monkey because of his tricks...
6. The animals went in seven by seven the little pig thought he was going to heaven...

Am C Am

1-6 And they all went into the ark for to get out of the rain.

Learn the song

Step 1

Listen to the song on tracks 2 & 3 of CD 2. Sing along to the music and learn the structure. Revise the three chords used in this song. Practise the chords individually and then play them in the correct order. Strum once or twice per chord. Line 3 is fairly difficult. Only strum once per chord or play the bass notes here (represented by the bold strings on the chord diagrams).

Step 2

Clap along to the song now. Notice that you are matching the tambourine sound on the recording as you clap. This is where you should aim to strum on the guitar - 1, 2, 3 & 4. Try playing the guitar with the performance track (02) now. At first only strum when you feel comfortable, maybe even one strum per chord, then work up to matching the tambourine, 1-2-3-4.

Step 3

Play to the performance or backing track, depending on whether or not you want to sing while you play. Try to play an easy, laid-back rhythm on the guitar to suit the piece.

All together now

- Discuss with the group the story of Noah's ark on which the song is obviously based. **Listen to the song and sing together**. For a performance, eg, for an assembly, divide the singers into pairs and each can dress up or paint a picture of the animal (from the lyrics) that they will represent. The rest of the group can be instrumentalists.
- This song sounds good when **lots of people are playing the guitar as they sing**, however, it can also be effective if only one person plays. First, listen again to the song. Ask everyone to walk on the spot as they sing. This walking pace is the natural pulse of the music and the rhythm that most instruments, including the guitar. will play.
- Now ask confident individuals to play the guitar along to the performance track (02) while everyone else sings. You may have to practise this at a slower pace without the CD first. Then play with the backing track (03).
- **Add a drummer to the performance**. A big deep bass drum sounds lovely, particularly as an introduction, as though the animals are being summoned by Noah.
- Coconut shells tapped together sound like the hooves of animals, which suits the story. The children might like to **make instruments out of bins, newspaper, junk or use their voices to make noises which represent the animals** in the story/song.

14 Amazing grace

4/5

Chords used in this song

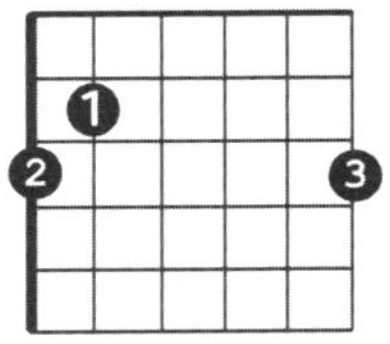

G major

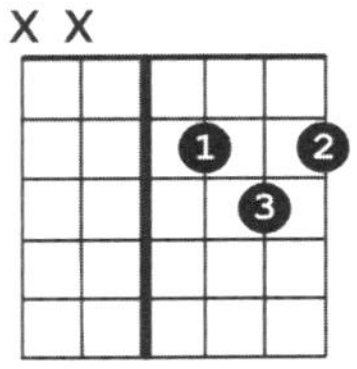

D major

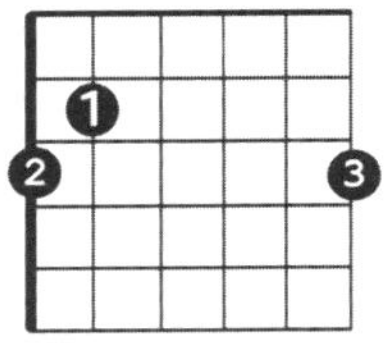

C major

Verse 1

G C G
Amazing grace, how sweet the sound,

G D
That saved a wretch like me.

G C G
I once was lost, but now am found,

G D G
Was blind, but now I see.

Verse 2

G C G
T'was grace that taught my heart to fear,

G D
And grace my fears relieved.

G C G
How precious did that grace appear,

G D G
The hour I first believed.

Repeat verse 1

Learn the song

Step 1

Revise the three chords used in this piece They are G major, C major and D major. Most of the changes are between G major and C major, so practise this change repeatedly until it is fluent. Also try playing only the bass notes, plucking once for each chord (see highlighted strings on the chord diagrams). This might be an easier way to practise playing the song, until you can manage the full chords.

Step 2

Listen to the performance track (4) until you are familiar with the tune and the song. Sing along to the CD.
If you are only playing the bass notes at this point, try to play some, or all, of the full chords.
Start by miming the chords along to the music, without strumming, and then slowly introduce strumming the chords. Strum once per chord to begin with.

Step 3

Now listen to the backing track (4) and sing only. Listen out for the guitarist on the recording and get a feel for when you should strum. Play the chords along to the backing track (5) and do not sing. Make sure that you change chords at the correct point. Try to strum exactly the same rhythm as the guitarist on the recording at first, and then create your own rhythms. As you become more comfortable with the chords, you can sing as you play.

All together now

- **Give some of the singers maracas to play.** Listen to the backing track. You can hear the shaking 1-2-3, 1-2-3 etc. Ask this group to play along to the backing track (05) until they are comfortable with the consistent percussion.
- At verse 2 in the backing **the tambourine joins the group**. It plays just on beat 1 of the 1-2-3, outlined by the maracas. Ask a smaller group, or perhaps even one member of the group to play this part.
- *Amazing grace* has lots of **backing vocals**. There are 'oh's' which you can hear on both tracks. Copy the backing vocals on the track (05) or create your own.
- The stronger vocalists can sing **solo parts** for this piece, or a couple might sing it as a duet. Bear in mind that it is quite a difficult song to sing well.
- Others can **play the chords or bass notes on the guitar** (see 'Learn the song' above and chord diagrams, pg, 34).

15 You really got me

06/07

Chords used in this song

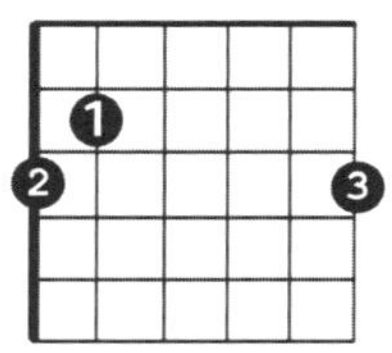

G major

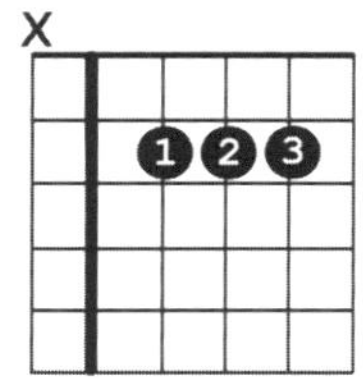

A major

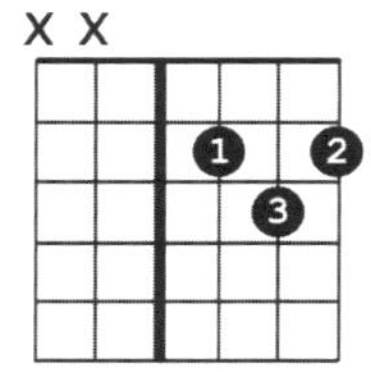

D major

G
Girl, you really got me goin,
You got me so I dont know what Im doin.
Yeah, you really got me now,
You got me so I cant sleep at night...

CHORUS:
A
Yeah, you really got me now.
You got me so I dont know what Im doin, now. Oh,
D
Yeah, you really got me now,
You got me so I cant sleep at night,
D
You really got me,
You really got me,
D   C
You really got me.
G
See, dont ever set me free,
I always wanna be by your side.
Girl, you really got me now,
You got me so I cant sleep at night...

CHORUS & GUITAR SOLO
G
See, dont ever set me free,
I always wanna be by your side.
Girl, you really got me now,
You got me so I cant sleep at night...

CHORUS:

Learn the song

Step 1

Listen to the performance track (06, CD 2) and the original. It is a famous song by British band, The Kinks, released in 1964. Sing along to the CD first and clap in time. Notice that you can count a slow 1-2, when you are clapping. Also hear the riff underneath, which copies the rhythm of the words 'you rea-lly got me'. You will learn this in Step 3. Another option is to only play the bass notes (see highlighted, bold strings on chord diagrams).

Step 2

Look at the chords. Start by playing the slow chords on the first, or '1' of the '1-2' that you counted in step 1.
The chords in this song are G major, A major and D major. Revisit other songs with these chords and practise changing from one chord to another. Listen to the performance and backing tracks (06/07, CD 2). Although the song is quite fast, these chords are strummed quite infrequently. Try to copy the guitar on the CD and sing as you play.

Step 3

To play the riff you must do the following:

• Your left hand only frets the 6th string (low E). The number represents the fret number (count from the tuning peg end of the guitar).
Fret:

You rea-lly got me

E 1 - 3 - 3 - 1 - 3

E 3 - 5 - 5 - 3 - 5,

E 8 - 10 - 10 - 8 - 10,

All together now

- First everyone should **learn the words and the melody**. Use the performance and backing tracks (06/07, CD 2) to do this, and clap in time to the music.
- Give some, or all, of the group a guitar if possible. Divide them into two halves. Some of the group **slowly strum the chords** while others play the 'you rea-lly got me' riff (see Step 3). Otherwise only one or two members of the group can play the guitar. Swap so that everyone has a chance to play.
- Listen to the backing track (07, CD 2). There is a lot of **percussion** that can easily be copied or enhanced for a group performance. Clapping and finger-clicks can be used effectively too. Give some of the singers woodblocks, maracas and drums. Copy the rhythms on the track or create original rhythms.
- If you have a capable guitarist or keyboard player, they could try to listen to the solo and play. Failing that, use the backing track (07, CD 2) or sing to the 'la' as a second vocal part. Listen out for other **backing vocals** on the CD and incorporate them into the performance.
- Allow the group to **experiment with the accompaniment**. Divide the group into little 'bands'. They can sing and play together without the CD using any instruments they choose. The 'bands' perform to one another. Discuss the different versions/interperatations of the song. How has it changed? What else could you do?

16 Scarborough Fayre

08/09

Chords used in this song

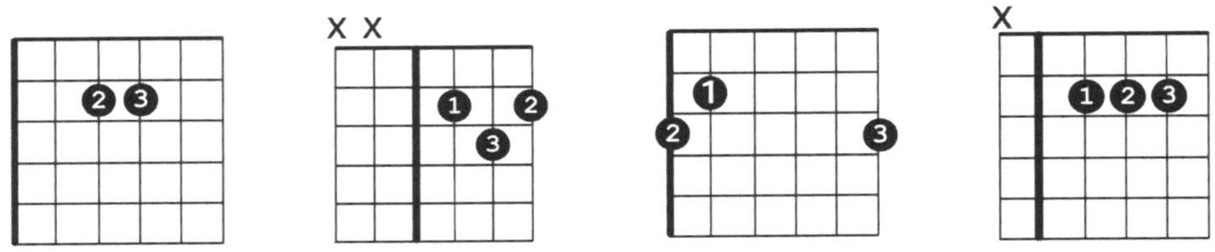

E minor D major G major A major

Em D Em

1. Are you going to Scarborough Fayre?
2. Tell her to make me a cambric shirt,
3. Tell her to find me an acre of land,
4. Tell her to reap it in a sickle of leather

G Em A Em

1. Parsley, sage, rosemary and thyme.
2. Parsley, sage, rosemary and thyme.
3. Parsley, sage, rosemary and thyme.
4. Parsley, sage, rosemary and thyme.

Em G D

1. Remember me to one who lives there,
2. Withoust no seams nor needle - work,
3. Between the salt water and the sea strand.
4. And to gather it all in a bunch of heather,

Em D Em

1. He once was a true love of mine.
2. Then she'll be a true love of mine.
3. Then she'll be a true love of mine.
4. Then she'll be a true love of mine.

REPEAT VERSE 1

Learn the song

Step 1

All four chords for *Scarborough Fayre* have been used before in this book. Revise the chords using the chord diagrams and other songs.
Mime the shapes of the chords, and practise changing between them, trying not to hesitate for a long time between changes.
Some sections of the song are quite difficult. You might wish to only play the bass notes/strings for these chords. Remember, the bass note for G major needs to be fretted with finger '2' (see diagram page 38).

Step 2

Listen to the song and sing using the lyrics (pg, 38). Notice when the guitar strums on the track.
Try practising each line separately without the CD, before attempting the entire song.
Only strum each chord once to begin with.
During line 2 ('Parsley, sage, rosemary and thyme') you may wish to play only the bass notes and practise the chords on their own without the CD until they can be played at the correct speed.

Step 3

Try playing the chords along to the performance track (08, CD 2) if it is not too fast. Notice how in verse 2 and 4 the guitarist strums more often on each chord. He strums in sets of three, 1-2-3, 1-2-,3, rather than once per chord. Try to copy this rhythm and play to the backing track (09).
Strum either the more complex rhythm, the simpler one, or a mixture of both as on the CD.
Once you can play and sing at the same time, perform without the CD and sing as a duet if possible.

All together now

- Ensure that every one can see the lyric and chord sheet (page 38). Ask the children to point out words that are unfamiliar. Find out together, or **explain the story of the lyrics** and the origins of the song.
- Listen to the performance track (31) as many times as necessary and **teach the song line by line**, and then verse by verse. Sing the whole song with the performance track. Divide the singers into two or more groups. One group can sing the part of the male voice on the CD and the other can sing the verses that the female sings. Some verses can be sung by everyone or they/you can create vocal harmonies.
- Give some of the group guitars or, failing that, only the leader or teacher can **play the guitar along with the singers**. The guitarist/s play while the others sing. They must try to keep in time with one another by listening and feeling the pulse. Allow them time to practise together away from the singers, with the CD. They must decide on the rhythm they will strum for each verse – each chord once, three times, or a mixture of both. Some guitarists might prefer to only play the bass notes (see highlighted strings on chord diagrams).
- **Shake tambourines or maracas** in time to the music 1-2-3, 1-2-3 or just on the first beat ('1'). If anyone in the group can play the flute, or piano, they can play the melody along with the voices. The melody line is on page 66.

A7

A7 is a rather easy chord to play, having only two notes fretted in the left hand. Make sure that your left hand fingers are pressed securely against the fretboard. This will ensure a nice tone. Do not strum the string (E) with the X above it. To play the bass note only, which is far easier, pluck the A open string as highlighted on the diagram. Notice that A7 is the A major chord without the middle finger. Practise moving from A major to A7, and back again.

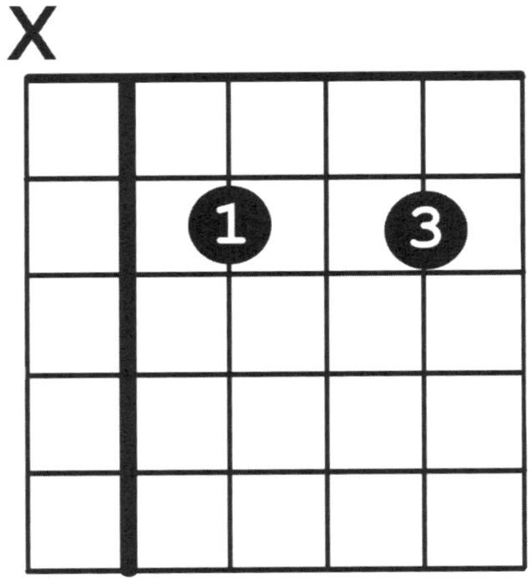

D7

D7 has three fretted notes in the left hand. Make sure that your left hand fingers are pressed securely against the fretboard. This will ensure a nice tone. Do not strum the strings (E and A) with the X's above them. To play only the bass note, which is far easier, pluck the D open string, as highlighted on the diagram. Notice that D7 is also triangular shaped, like D major.

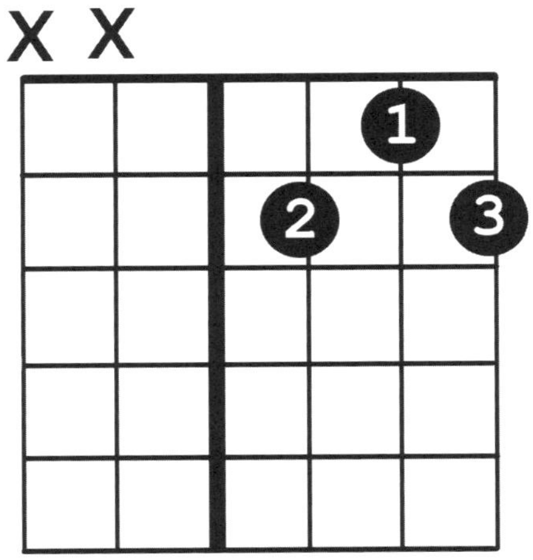

F major

There is an easy and a more difficult way to play the F major chord: Both are explained on this page. Of course start by playing the easier version. The more difficult shape involves a technique called 'barring'. As you progress on the guitar, barring becomes more common (explanation below).
First, for the easier option, make sure that finger 1 covers both of the two highest strings (B and E) firmly. If you wish to play only the root/bass note of the chord to begin with. Play only the D string (highlighted on the diagram) with the third finger fretting the third fret, as shown. Do not strum the two strings with X above them.

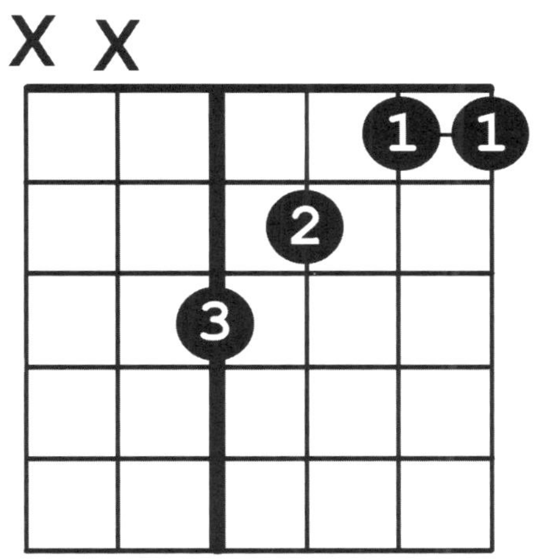

F major

To play F major using barring, press all the strings behind the first fret with finger 1 (see diagram). You finger acts as an artificial nut and raises the pitch of all the strings by one note. Thereafter the chord shape is the same as the chord of E. This procedure is called barring. It is not easy and needs strong fingers. Only those who feel absolutely happy with the chords so far should attempt this. Practise the chord many times.

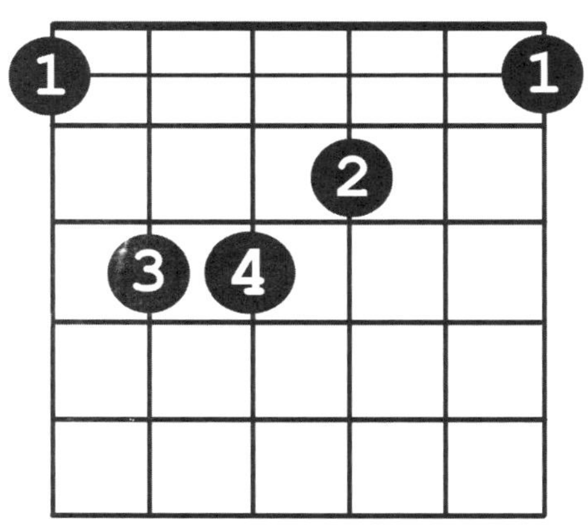

F major (barred)

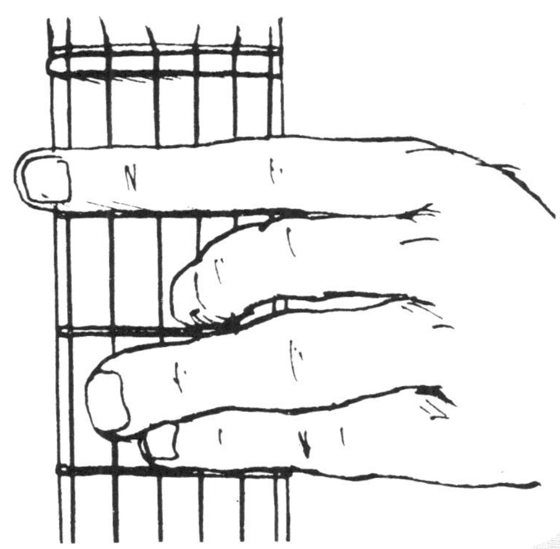

Hand position for F major (barred)

17 Head, shoulders knees and toes

10/11

Chords used in this song

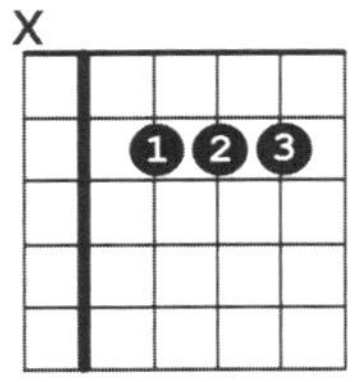

A major

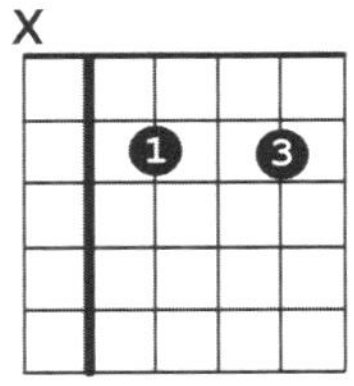

A7

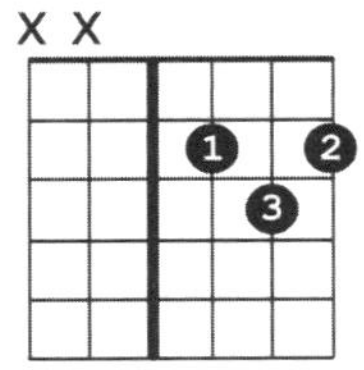

D major

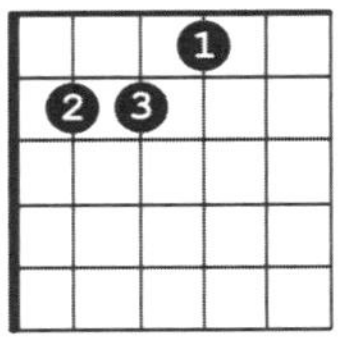

E major

	A	A	A	A
1.	Head,	shoulders, knees and	toes, knees and	toes,
2.	Stretch up	high, then to the	ground, to the	ground,
3.	Bend your	knees, jump up and	down, up and	down,
4.	Head,	shoulders, knees and	toes, knees and	toes,

	A	A	E	E
1.	Head,	shoulders, knees and	toes, knees and	toes, and
2.	Stretch up	high, then to the	ground, to the	ground, now
3.	Bend your	knees, jump up and	down, up and	down, then
4.	Head,	shoulders, knees and	toes, knees and	toes, and

	A	A7	D	D
1.	Eyes, and	ears, and	mouth and	nose,
2.	Hands on	hips and	spin a -	round,
3.	Stamp your	feet and	make a	frown,
4.	Eyes, and	ears, and	mouth and	nose,

	E	E	A	A
1.	Head,	shoulders, knees and	toes, knees and	toes.
2.	Stretch up	high, then to the	ground, to the	ground
3.	Bend your	knees, jump up and	down, up and	down
4.	Head,	shoulders, knees and	toes, knees and	toes.

Learn the song

Step 1

Revise the chords used in the song, particularly the new chord A7 (pg, 40). The first line of each verse is manageable, however it then changes rather quickly, particularly in line 3, where you might only wish to play the bass notes to begin with (see highlighted strings on chord diagrams).
Practise these chords/bass notes slowly, without the CD, until confident.

Step 2

Listen to the performance track (10, CD 2) and then the backing track (11, CD 2). Listen out for the guitar. Clap along to the music. The claps symbolise when you should strum the chords. Try to play the chords with the CD. Follow the chords on pg, 42.
Learn the lyrics. When you feel comfortable, play and sing the whole song slowly without the CD.

Step 3

The guitarist on the CD strums the 'offbeat.' This means that of the 1-2-3-4 beats clapped, a downstrum is played on the 2 and the 4, rather than the 1 and the 3. Keep listening to the performance track (10) and try to copy the guitarist's strumming rhythm. Finally sing and play to the speed of the backing track (11).

All together now

- Make sure that **everyone in the group knows the song and the lyrics (pg, 42)**. The lyrics have been changed from the conventional verses, however the first verse is still the same.
- **Make the actions as you sing**. Follow the lyrics (pg, 42).
- **Introduce some guitars** or the leader can play the guitar. It is helpful though if the leader is demonstrating the actions while everyone sings. Choose some children to **clap in time** on the strong beats. If they can manage it, ask them to clap the offbeat (you can hear this clapping pattern on the backing track (11)
- Sing once without anyone doing the actions but with **everyone playing the guitar and singing**. Some might play only the bass notes (see highlighted strings on chord diagrams, pg, 42). Make clear to the group that they play on the second and fourth counts. To demonstrate this it is effective to play the backing track; point out the strumming, and then copy it). This rhythmic pattern is quite complex and will need practice. Keep listening to the CD tracks for clarity.

18 If you're happy and you know it

12/13

Chords used in this song

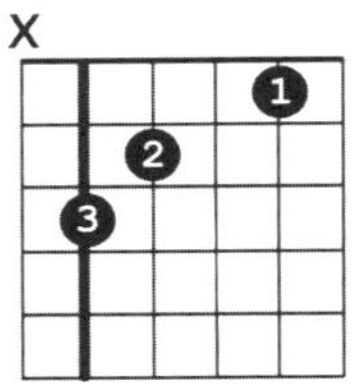

C major

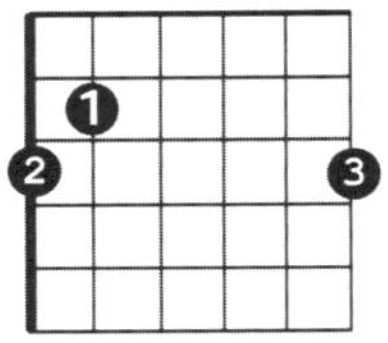

G major

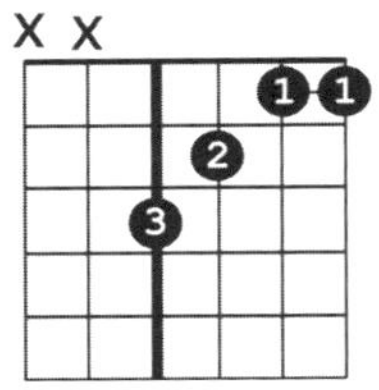

F major

C	G

1. If you're happy and you know it, clap your hands (clap clap),
2. If you're happy and you know it, stamp your feet (stamp stamp),
3. If you're happy and you know it, strum the chords (strum strum),
4. If you're happy and you know it, tap the beat (tap tap),
5. If you're happy and you know it sing hooray (horray!),

G | C

1. If you're happy and you know it, clap your hands (clap clap),
2. If you're happy and you know it, stamp your feet (stamp stamp),
3. If you're happy and you know it, strum the chords (strum strum),
4. If you're happy and you know it, tap the beat (tap tap),
5. If you're happy and you know it sing hooray (horray!),

F | C

1. If you're happy and you know it, and you really want to show it,
2. If you're happy and you know it, and you really want to show it,
3. If you're happy and you know it, and you really want to show it,
4. If you're happy and you know it and you really want to show it,
5. If you're happy and you know it and you really want to show it,

G | C

1. If you're happy and you know it, clap your hands (clap clap),
2. If you're happy and you know it, stamp your feet (stamp stamp),
3. If you're happy and you know it, strum the chords (strum strum)

G C

4. If you're happy and you know it, tap the beat (tap tap).
5. If you're happy and you know it sing hooray (horray!).

Learn the song

Step 1

Look at page 41. Find the F Major chord on the guitar and practise it until you are sure of its position. Change from C to F, and G to F, and back again. If the F major chord is too difficult, play only the bass note. To do this strum the highlighted string on the diagram with finger '3' fretted as shown. A full explanation of the F major chord is on pg, 41.

Step 2

Listen to the performance track (12, CD 2) and look at the lyric and chord page (pg, 44). Sing the song with the CD. Memorise the order of chords as they are not written out for each verse. Each chord is strummed once on the strong beat.
Notice that you do not play in the introduction. With the CD, mime the chords along to the music and then begin to strum the chords.

Step 3

Practise slowly without the CD until you are ready to increase the pace and play along to the performance or backing tracks. Sing as you play. Strum a rhythm that you find comfortable. First, listen to the guitar on the CD and then copy it until you feel comfortable to try other strumming rhythms.

All together now

- **Sing the song together**. One or more of you can play the guitar or you can all just sing along to the CD.
- **Make the actions as you sing**. Remember to clap in the right place, stamp your feet and pretend to strum the chords.
- Everyone can now try to **sing and play the guitar** (without actions). Use the backing track (13) if it is easier, or just play slowly without the CD.
- Give some singers **tambourines** to shake in time and a drummer can keep a steady beat.
- Make up your own verses and actions, and have others in the group make up verses too:

eg, **If you're happy and you know it wave hello (wave, wave)**
If you're grumpy and you know it, pull a frown (frown, frown)
If you're hungry and you know it, eat a cake (yum yum)

19 Jingle bells

14/15

Chords used in this song

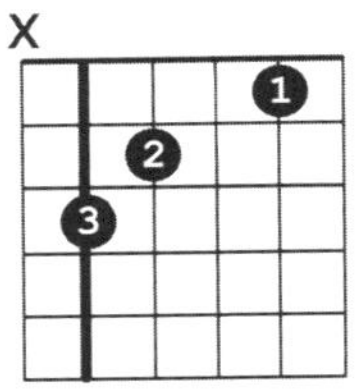

C major

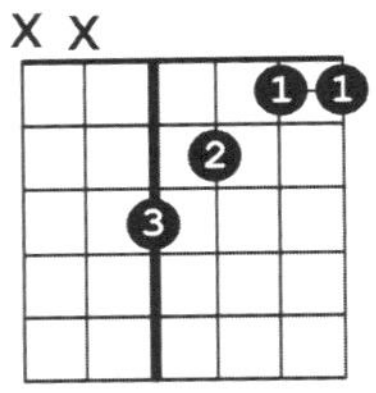

F major

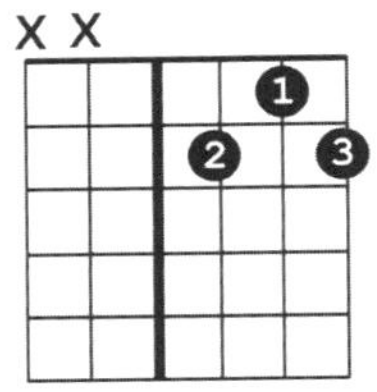

D7

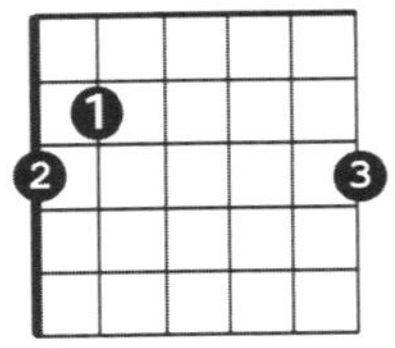

G major

VERSE:

C F
Dashing through the snow, In a one horse open sleigh.

F G C
Over fields we go, laughing all the way.

C F
Bells on bob tails ring, making spirits bright,

F G C
Oh what fun it is to sing a sleighing song tonight....Oh!

CHORUS:

C
Jingle bells, jingle bells, jingle all the way.

F C D7 G
Oh, what fun it is to ride, in a one horse open sleigh. Hey!

C
Jingle bells, jingle bells, jingle all the way.

F C G C
Oh, what fun it is to ride, in a one horse open sleigh.

REPEAT VERSE AND CHORUS x 2

Learn the song

Step 1

Jingle bells does not use any new chords, however F major is played more often so it is essential that you are happy with the chord. Play it repeatedly. Revise G major and C major also, as they are played in the song. Practise changing chords between F, C and G without the CD. Line 2 of the verse is quite difficult. To begin with, play the bass notes only (see highlighted strings and notes on chord diagrams).

Step 2

Listen to the performance track (14). This version has both the chorus and the verse. Make sure that you know each one and practise singing using the lyrics (page 46). As you sing, imagine or mime when you would strum and change chords.

Clap or count in time to the music (1-2-3-4). This is the natural pulse. Where you are clapping or counting is where you are aiming to strum, however you can strum less often to begin with.

Step 3

Play the chords without the CD, strumming four chords per line. Try to sing as you play if possible, with either of the CD tracks. Listen to the rhythm that the guitarist is strumming on the CD and copy.

Try to play with a reggae style like the CD. Play an upstrum on the offbeats (so strum on the '2' and '4' of the '1-2-3-4' count).

All together now

- Divide the group. Some can sing the verse or take turns singing the verse, and **everyone can sing** the chorus together. Failing that, everyone can sing the whole song. It is a jolly Christmas song so the more energy the better.
- Group members or the leader can play the guitar. If everyone is playing the guitar, ensure that you practise many times without any vocals. One person can sing so that the guitarists remember the melody as they play.
- **Give some singers bells to shake during the performance**. Make sure that they play them at a regular pace 1-2-3-4. This will help the guitarists to know when they should strum. Afterwards, the percussionists should try to create an original rhythm to enhance the performance. They might shake the rhythm 'Jin-gle bells' with a 'quick quick slow' pattern consistently throughout the song. Practise alone with the CD. before joining the vocalists and guitaritsts.
- On the CD (chorus) you will hear a descending scale. **Give some of the group xylophones, chime bars or glockenspiels**. Others might wish to play it on a keyboard. It is simply a C major scale descending - C' B A G F E D C - repeatedly in time to the music. Pick it out on the CD and copy it.

20 Oh when the saints

16/17

Chords used in this song

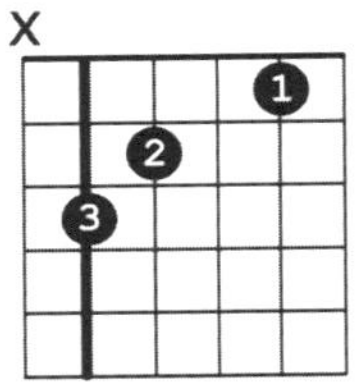

C major

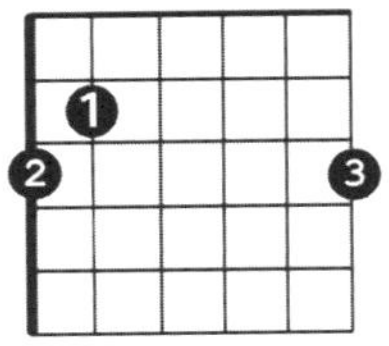

G major

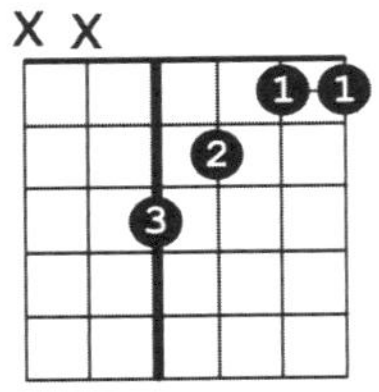

F major

C

1. Oh when the saints, go marching in,
2. Oh when the band begin to play,
3. Oh when the bells begin to ring,
4. Oh when the stars refuse to shine,
5. Oh when the saints go marching in,

G

1. Oh when the saints go marching in,
2. Oh when the band be- gin to play,
3. Oh when the bells be- gin to ring,
4. Oh when the stars re-fuse to shine,
5. Oh when the saints go marching in,

C F

1. I want to be in that number,
2. I want to be in that number,
3. I want to be in that number,
4. I want to be in that number,
5. I want to be in that number,

C G C

1. Oh when the saints go marching in.
2. Oh when the band be-gin to play.
3. Oh when the bells be-gin to ring.
4. Oh when the stars re- fuse to shine.
5. Oh when the saints go marching in.

Learn the song

Step 1

Look at the chords in this piece – C, G and F major. Again, there are no new chords here, although there are difficult changes (eg, C to F in line 3). Slowly play through the chords without the CD. Next, listen to the CD. If the chords are too difficult, play only the bass notes (represented by the highlighted strings and notes on the chord diagrams).

Step 2

Now listen to the performance track again (16, CD 2) and sing along using the lyric sheet on pg, 48. Clap in time to the music. The places where you clap are the strong beats, where you should try to downstrum.
Mime or play with the music. Try to change quickly enough to keep in time with the track. If this is not possible at first, play without the music or strum less frequently.

Step 3

Try more original strum rhythms. Rather than only playing a downstrum on the strong beat, experiment with creating a 'richer' accompaniment by adding more upstrums. Listen to the guitar on the recording and copy some of the more unusual, jazzy (syncopated) strumming that you hear.

All together now

- Vocalists can **sing the whole song together**, divide the verses, or work on a 'question and answer' structure. To do this, divide the group into two: Group 1 sing the first line and group 2 echo it. They do the same for the second line.
  Then they sing the last two lines together (see below).
  Try this without the CD.
- Eg,

Group 1	**Group 2**
Oh when the saints	(Oh when the saints)
Go marching in	(Go marching in)

  Together
  Oh when the saints go marching in.
  I want to be in that number,
  Oh when the saints go marching in.
- Some, or all, of the group can **play the guitar and sing.** At first play the chords only, or with the performance tracks. If the vocalists are divided (as above), only use a small group of guitarists. Otherwise the guitarists will overwhelm the singing.
- **Give some of the singers drums to beat time with**. Can they try to open the song with a drum roll? The drummers can march on the spot as they perform like a marching band. Give some other members of the group tambourines to shake in time to the music
- This is a simple melody and **can be learnt on the keyboard or tuned percussion**.
  The melody line is on page 68.

21 You are my sunshine

18/19

Chords used in this song

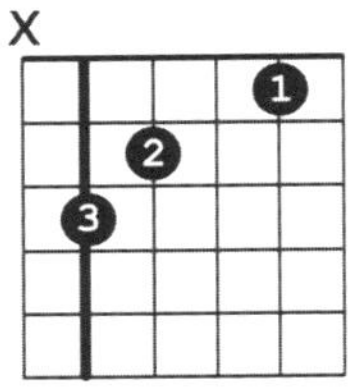

C major

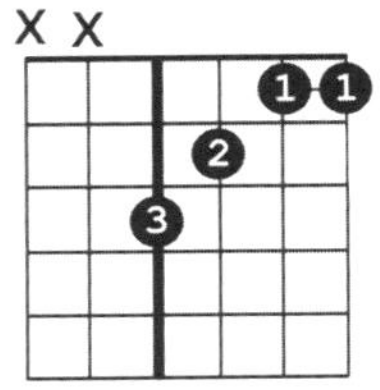

F major

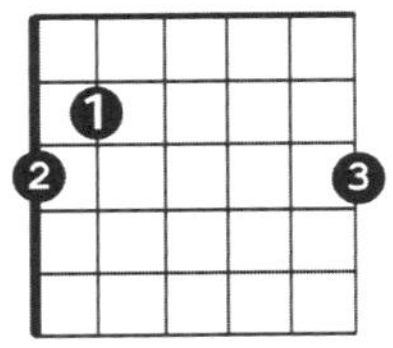

G major

C

1. You are my sunshine, my only sunshine,
2. The other nite, dear, as I lay sleeping,
3. Louis - i - ana, my Louisiana,
4. You are my sunshine, my only sunshine,

F C

1. You make me happy, when skies are grey.
2. I dreamed I held you in my arms.
3. The place where I was, , where I was born.
4. You make me happy, when skies are grey.

F C

1. You'll never know, dear, how much I love you,
2. When I awoke, dear, I was mistaken,
3. White fields of cotton, green fields of clover,
4. You'll never know, dear, how much I love you,

C G C

1. Please don't take my sunshine away.
2. And I hung my head and cried.
3. The best fishing and long tall corn.
4. Please don't take my sunshine away.

Learn the song

Step 1

Again this song has the three chords C major, Fmajor and G major. Before you play the chords, it is worth only playing the bass notes, represented by the highlighted (bold) strings on the chord diagram. The bass notes for C major and G major have a left-hand fretted note. Try to sing along as you play the bass notes.

Step 2

Now play the chords in the correct order without the CD. Try to sing along as you play. If you do not know the tune, listen to the performance track (18, CD 2) until you are certain of the melody. Pay particular attention to the changes and practise them slowly without the CD. Listen to the backing track (19) for the strumming rhythms. The guitarist plays on the offbeat. Try to copy exactly what you hear on the CD.

Step 3

Now play the chords along to the song. Make the rhythm interesting by strumming on the offbeat (see step 2). Try strumming 1-2-3-4 along to the natural pulse of the song too, which might be slightly easier. Work towards singing and playing together at the same speed as the backing track, or sing and play without the CD.

All together now

- **All sing together.** This song does not suit many vocal parts or harmonies. At the most some singers can make up harmonies ('oo') in the last verses. It is fun to sing in a country accent (like on CD 2, track 18). Perhaps pick out some lines for solos (such as 'the other night dear, as I lay sleepin, I dreamed I held you, in my arms').
- **Discuss the lyrics.** Who is singing the song and what happens? Ask the group to mirror the sentiment of the story in their singing, they might sound upset or get quieter for the 'hung my head and cried' line for example.
- Have **some of the group play the guitar part** (see steps 1-3). If they need to practise alone or with the CD let them do so. Only once the guitarists are confident should you add the singers. Do not attempt to sing too quickly, but at a pace that the guitarists can manage.
- **Add percussionists now**: Use coconut shells/woodblocks to tap out a rhythm that sounds like the 'clip clop' of a horse, to suit the cowboy feel. Maybe add a relaxed rhythm, shaken on maracas or a tambourine (listen to the CD). Urge the group to **experiment with rhythmic accompaniments** using the instruments available.

22 House of the rising sun

20/21

Chords used in this song

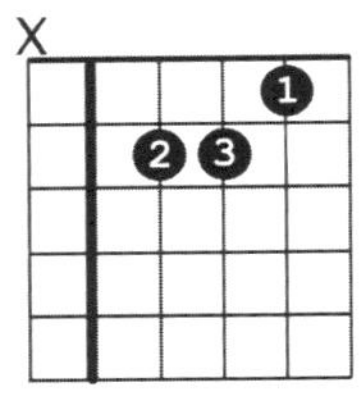

A minor

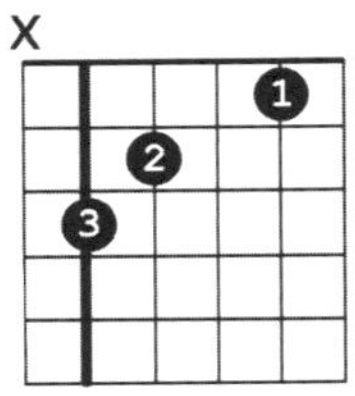

C major

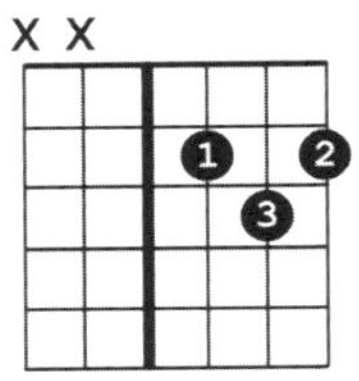

D major

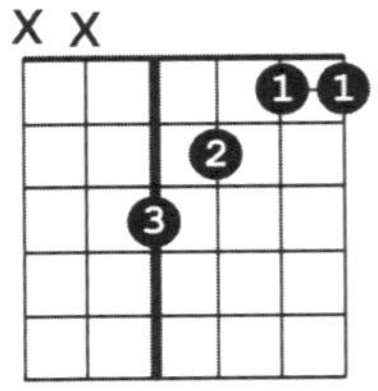

F major

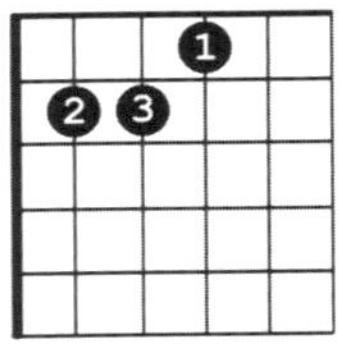

E major

	Am	C	D		F
1.	There is a	house in	New	Orleans,	
2.	My mother	was a	tailor,		
3.	Oh mother	tell your	children,		
4.	There is a	house in	New	Orleans,	

		Am	C	E
1.	They	call the	Rising	Sun.
2.	She	sewed my	new blue	jeans.
3.	Not to do	what	I have	done.
4.	They	call the	Rising	Sun.

			Am		C		D			F
1.	And	it's	been	the	ruin	of	many	a	poor	boy,
2.	My		father		was	a	gamblin'			man,
3.	Spend	your	lives	in	sin	and	mis -	e	-	ry,
4.	And	it's	been	the	ruin	of	many	a	poor	boy

		Am		E		Am	E
1.	And	God	I	know	I'm	one.	
2.		Down in		New	Or -	leans.	
3.	In the	House of the Rising				Sun.	
4.	And	God	I	know	I'm	one.	

Learn the song

Step 1

House of the rising sun is a famous traditional song which was covered by a band called The Animals.
Here we are revisiting some of the chords from earlier on in the book – there are lots of chords used and they change after just one strum.
This will need a lot of practice before you can attempt it with the CD.
Listen to the performance track (20, CD 2) and pay attention to where you can hear the guitar.

Step 2

Without the CD practise the chords one after the other – Amin, C major, D major and F major. Listen to the CD tracks to learn the rhythm. Then, when you are feeling confident, play along to the performance track (20).
At least once put down your guitar and only sing along to the music. Feel the natural pulse as you sing, or step from foot to foot in time to the music.

Step 3

Play the whole song at a slow pace. SIng while you play if possible. Once the chord changes are fluent, try to sing as you play. When confident, play with the performance track (20) and finally sing with the backing track (21).
Notice in later verses, that the guitar plays each chord quickly six times before changing. Try this slowly at first and then build the speed.

All together now

- **First everyone learns the song and lyrics**. Listen to the performance track many times and maybe play the group the original version too. Teach it verse by verse, repeating lines and using the CD. Notice the change in pitch (high or low) that happens with the vocal is doubled. Divide the group. Some children can sing the higher part and the rest can sing the lower part.
- **All or some of the group can play the guitar**. Ensure that the singers and the guitarists have decided on a speed that they can manage. Otherwise, the guitarists will be left behind.
- **Learn about the blues.** *House of the rising sun* is a traditional song which has been sung in a blues style. Learn about the origins of blues, listen to other blues music, and ask individuals to choose their favourite blues songs.

The chord of B7

B7 uses four fingers so may require some practice. Do not play the E string (it has an X above it). Make sure that all fingers are pressed securely against the fret board. This will ensure a nice tone. Do not strum the string (E) with the X above it. To play the bass note only which is easier, pluck the A string as highlighted on the diagram with finger 2 on the second fret (as below).

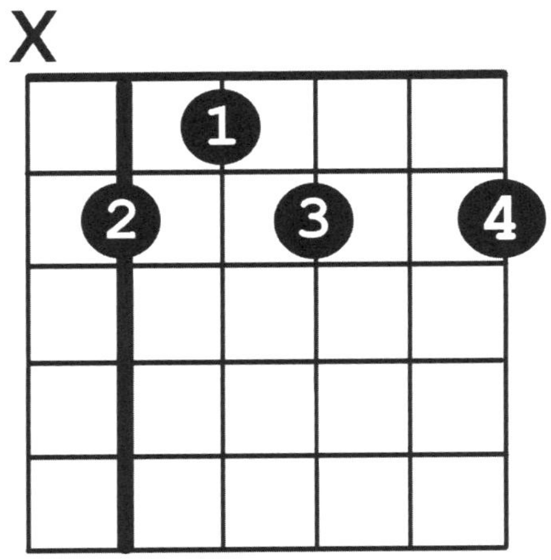

The chord of Dm

Below is the chord diagram for D minor. Do not strum the two strings with the X's above them (E and A). To play only the bass note, strum the open string which is highlighted on the diagram below.

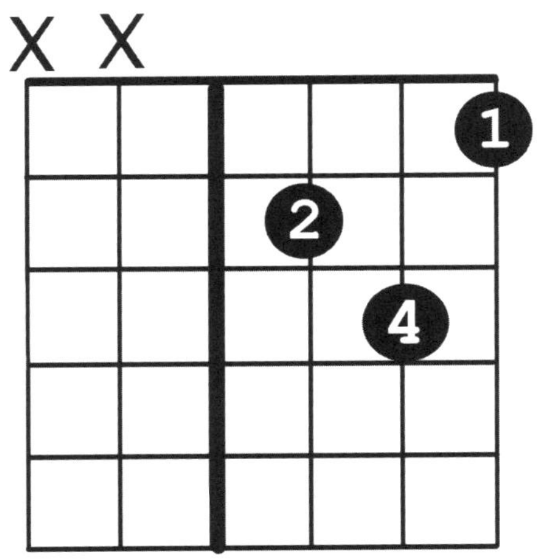

23 Daisy Bell

Chords used in this song

22/23

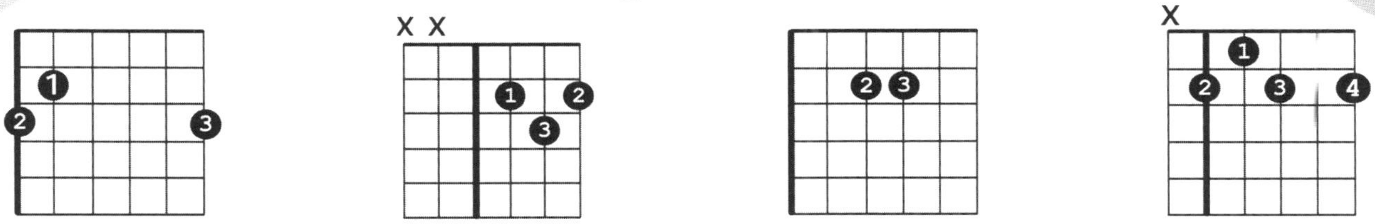

G major   D major   E minor   B7

CHORUS:

```
G                C                         G
Daisy, Daisy, give me your answer do.
D          G       A                      D
I'm half crazy, all for the love of you.
  D                        G
It won't be a stylish marriage,
 G
I can't afford a carriage,
     G            D          G          D
But you'll look sweet, upon the seat of a
G       D          G
Bicycle made for two.
```

VERSE 1

```
G                          D                   D      G
There is a flower within my heart, Daisy, Daisy!
G                             D
Planted one day by a glancing dart,
G              D      G
Planted by Daisy Bell!
```

Em B7 Em
Whether she loves me or loves me not,
D G
Sometimes it's hard to tell;
Em B7 Em
Yet I am longing to share the lot of a
A D
Beautiful Daisy Bell!

CHORUS

VERSE 2
G D D G
We will go tandem as man and wife, Daisy, Daisy.
G D
Peddlin' away down the road of life,
G D G
I and my Daisy Bell,

Em B7 Em
When the road's dark we can both despise,
D G
P'licemen and lamps as well;
Em B7 Em
There are bright lights in their dazzling eyes, of a
A D
Beautiful Daisy Bell.

CHORUS

Learn the song

Step 1

Learn the chord B7 (page 54). Repeatedly practise the change from Eminor to B7 and back again, which happens for 'Whether she loves me or loves me not.' It is a quick change and needs to be focused on and practised separately.
In fact there are many quick changes in this song. Another one is the G D G change for, 'Planted by Daisy Bell.'

Practise the changes slowly.

Step 2

Listen to the performance track (22, CD 2) and notice how quickly the chords change. Follow the lyric and chord sheet as you play (pg, 56). Play bass notes only if easier (highlighted strings on chord diagrams).
Without the CD try to play the song two lines at a time. Keep repeatedly practising the song in small sections before you attempt the whole thing. Play very slowly without the CD.

Step 3

Only when you are ready, try singing as you play, or try playing along to the performance or backing track. (22/23, CD 2)
Copy exactly the rhythm that the guitarist strums on the CD. You might find it easier to listen to the backing track (23) as it is easier to hear the guitar part.

All together now

- **Teach everyone the song**. Although the chorus is quite well-known, many people are not as familiar with the verse. Use the performance track to teach this (22) and teach it line by line if you need to.
  You can divide the verse into sections and have smaller groups sing them.
  There is a flower within my heart (group 1) Daisy, Daisy (group 2)
  Planted one day by a glancing dart (group 1)
  Planted by Daisy bell (group 2)
  Whether she loves me or loves me not (group 1)
  Sometimes it's hard to tell (group 2)
  But I am willing to share the lot (group 1)
  With my beautiful Daisy bell (2)
  Everyone sings the chorus together
- **Add tuned percussion** now eg, xylophones, chime bars and glockenspiel. They can play the notes above the lyrics in the chorus.
- **Everyone or just the leader plays the guitar.** Play bass notes only if it is too difficult (see steps above).
- **Add drums or tambourines** for the whole song or just the chorus.
  A good rhythm for the percussion is to play on the second and third beats of the bar.

1 x x 1 x x

24 My Bonnie lies over the ocean

24/25

Chords used in this song

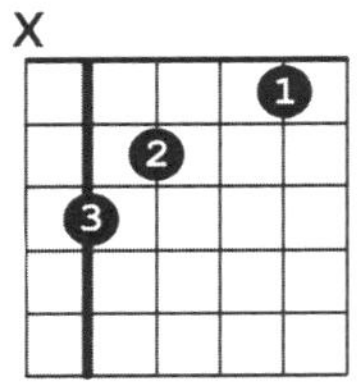

C major

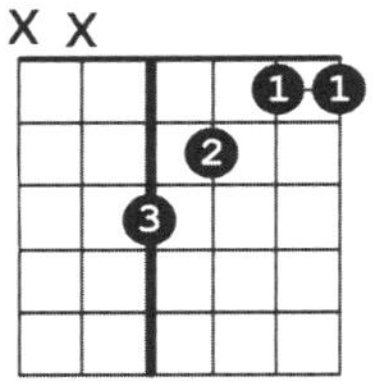

F major

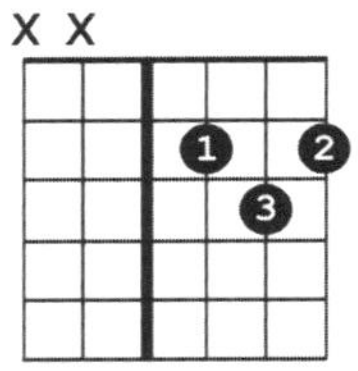

D major

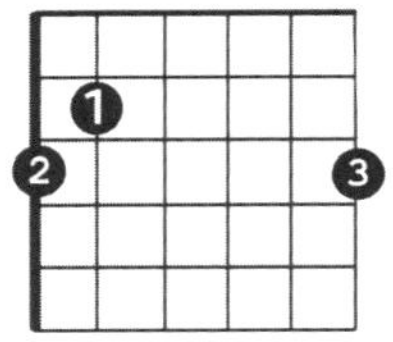

G major

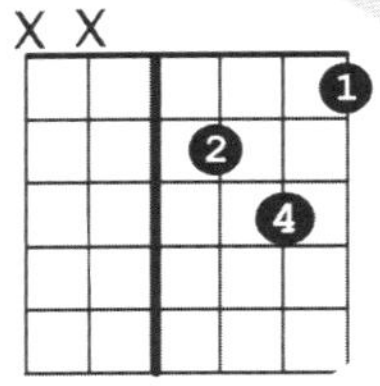

D minor

```
         C                                F            C
1. My    Bonnie    lies                   over   the   ocean,
2. Last  night     as   I                 lay  on my   pillow,
3. The   winds have blown                 over the     ocean,

         C                                D        G
1. My    Bonnie           lies            over the  sea.
2. Last  night     as     I               lay on my bed.
3. The   winds have       blown           over  the sea.

         C                                F             C         A
1. My    Bonnie    lies                   over   the    ocean,
2. Last  night     as   I                 lay  on my    pillow,
3. The   winds have  blown                over the      ocean,

          Dm                    G             C
1. Oh    bring back my         Bonnie to     me. (repeat verse 1)
2. I     dreamed that my Bonnie was dead.
3. And   brought back my Bonnie   to  me.
```

Chorus (after every verse, except the first)

```
C              F    D      G                         C
Bring back, bring back oh, bring back my Bonnie to me, to me.

C              F    D      G                         C
Bring back, bring back oh, bring back my  Bonnie to me.
```

Learn the song

For such a traditional favourite, this song has quite a few chords in it!
The track is *My Bonnie lies over the ocean* with a difference. It is a lively rock n roll version, which is reminiscent of the first time that The Beatles were ever recorded. They were the backing band for Tony Sheridan (you can look on youtube for this footage).
Do not be disheartened from playing this song because it speeds up. If you listen to the performance track (24) you will hear that actually the chords are played rather slowly, and each chord is only strummed once. There are still however quite frequent changes which need special attention.

Step 1

Learn the new chord (D minor, page 54) and practise changing from C to D minor and then from D to G, as this happens in the song. Revise the other chords in the song – C F G and D.

Step 2

Listen to the performance track (24, CD 2) and look at the lyrics and chords. The chords happen in little cycles of three. Practise these separately first
C F C
C D G
and
Dm G C
Get used to moving between chords.

Step 3

Try playing the cycles of chords in order now, to create a song. Add the extra chords. Practise until you can manage them quite fluently. When ready, play and sing along to the backing track (25) or to the performance track (24).

All together now

- **Learn the song** if you do not know it already. Use the performance track (24) to do so and practise it verse by verse.
  It is best if everyone sings the whole song, rather than dividing the vocalists into sections. At the most some children can create some harmonies ('oo's') to sing over the chorus ('bring back, bring back' etc), or a smaller group of soloists can sing the chorus by themselves (they can sing two lines each).
- **Add a small group of guitarists** to play the chords, or the leader can play. Some guitarists can just play the bass notes (see highlighted strings/notes on chord diagrams).
- **Dress up in rock and roll dress** if it is for a performance. It is fun to start slowly and then surprise the audience when it turns into a lively rock 'n' roll number!

25 I can see clearly now the rain is gone

26/27

Chords used in this song

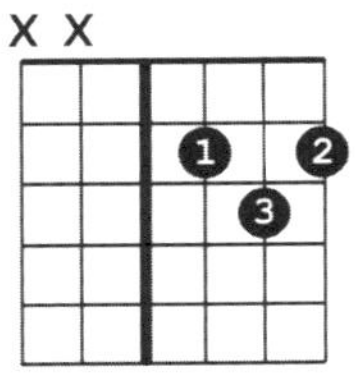
D major

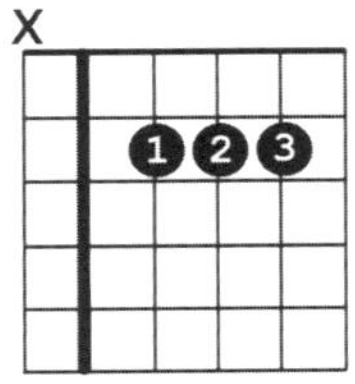
A major

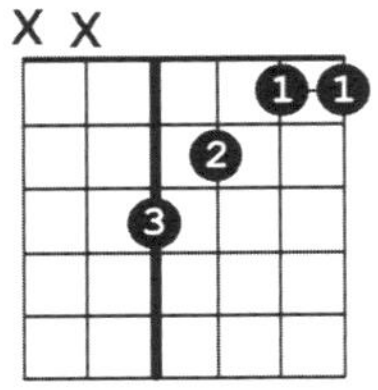
F major

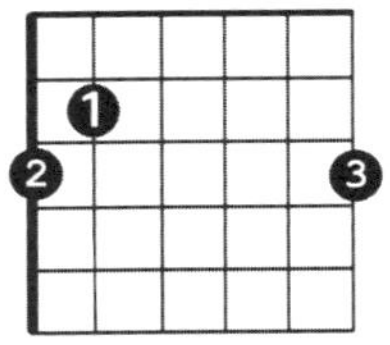
G major

D			G			D
1. I	**can**	**see**	**clearly**	**now,**	**the**	**rain is gone,**
2. I	**think I**	**can**	**make it**	**now,**	**the**	**pain is gone,**
3. I	**can**	**see**	**clearly**	**now,**	**the**	**rain is gone,**

D			G			A
1. I	**can**	**see**	**all**	**obstacles**		**in my way.**
2. All	**of**	**the**	**bad**	**feelings**	**have**	**disappeared.**
3. I	**can**	**see**	**all**	**obstacles**		**in my way.**

D			G			D
1. Gone	**are**	**the**	**dark**	**clouds**	**that**	**had me blind,**
2. Here	**is**	**the**	**rainbow**	**I've**	**been**	**prayin' for,**
3. Gone	**are**	**the**	**dark**	**clouds**	**that**	**had me blind,**

D			C		G
1. It's gonna	**be**	**a**	**bright**	**(bright),**	**bright (bright),**
2. It's gonna	**be**	**a**	**bright**	**(bright),**	**bright (bright),**
3. It's gonna	**be**	**a**	**bright**	**(bright),**	**bright (bright),**

G			D
1. Sun	**-**	**Shiny**	**day. (x2)**
2. Sun	**-**	**Shiny**	**day. (x2)**
3. Sun	**-**	**Shiny**	**day. (x4 to end).**

BRIDGE:

F C
Look all around, there's nothin' but blue skies,

F A
Look straight ahead, nothin' but blue skies.

Learn the song

This is a famous reggae song by Jimmy Cliff. Listen to the performance track if you are not familiar with it or find the original. The 'is' instead of 'has' in the title is intentional - it is Jamaican slang.

Step 1

The chords used in this song are D G F and A major. Revise these chords and practise changing from one chord to another slowly. Focus on it a line at a time and practise in small sections.

Step 2

Try to play along to the performance track (26, CD 2). At first just mime the chords as you listen. Slowly work on playing all of the chords. You can just strum each chord once to begin with.

Step 3

Try to add rhythm to the strumming now and play the whole song. Listen to the performance and backing tracks (26/27). Try to copy the rhythm played by the guitar. It is a typical syncopated reggae rhythm (you will hear how it strums on the offbeat). Listen to the backing track and copy the guitar rhythms.

All together now

- This is a great, upbeat song to **sing at a performance**, and it has a lovely positive image. Teach the song and study the lyrics. Talk about the meaning of the song. The rain, the sun and the blue skies are all metaphors for happiness after a bleak period.
- **Listen to other reggae songs**. You might choose Bob Marley or more by Jimmy Cliff. Talk about the elements that make it reggae and what we associate with reggae music – what does it make you think of? Happiness, sunshine, holidays, peace.
- **Add vocal harmonies**. Listen to the performance on track 49. There are many different vocal lines, particularly in the last chorus. You can choose to add them at any point, or make up your own harmonies.
- Some of the group can **play the guitar chords along to the music**. Others can **play percussion**. Drums, bells and tambourines do not really suit this song, but maracas & guiros do.
- You might **create some simple hand actions to accompany the song** for those who are not playing instruments. Also, have the children **paint some pictures to represent the song**, which might be used as a backdrop to a performance.

1 Row, row, row your boat

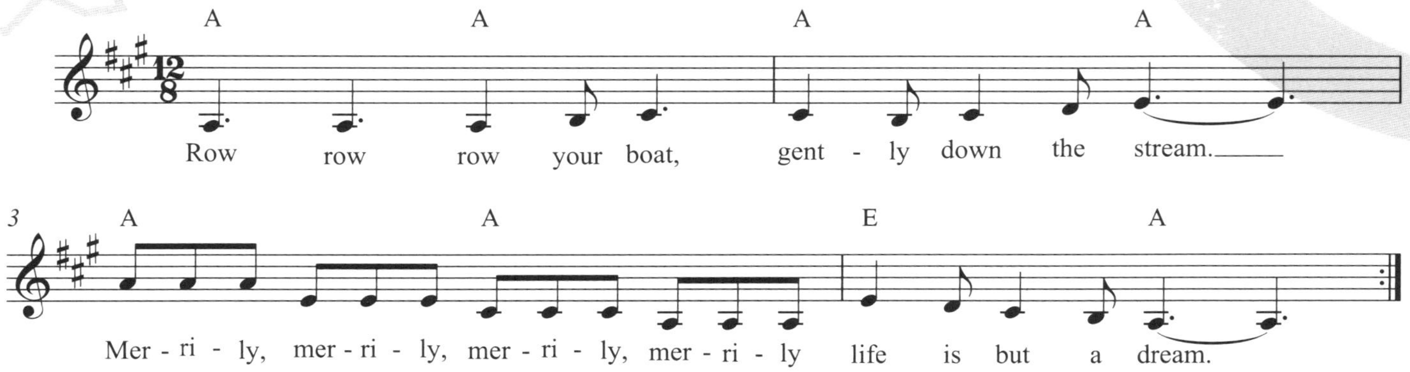

2 Ten in a bed

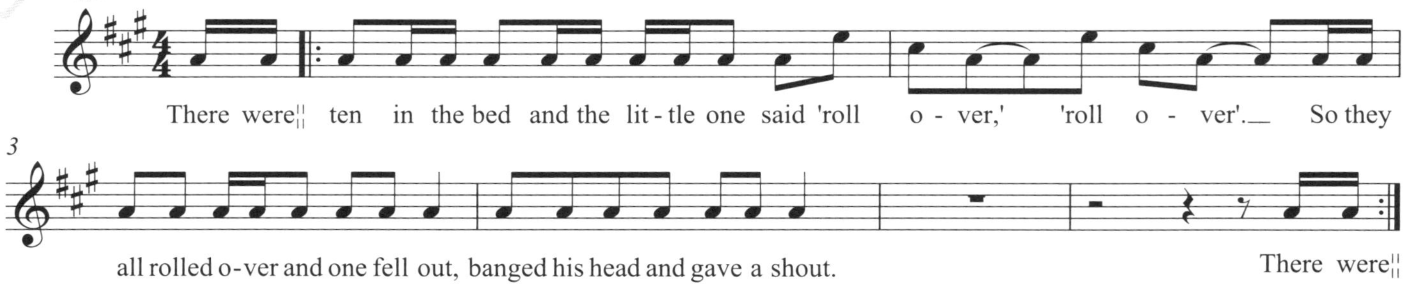

3 He's got the whole world in his hands

4 London's burning

5 Silent night

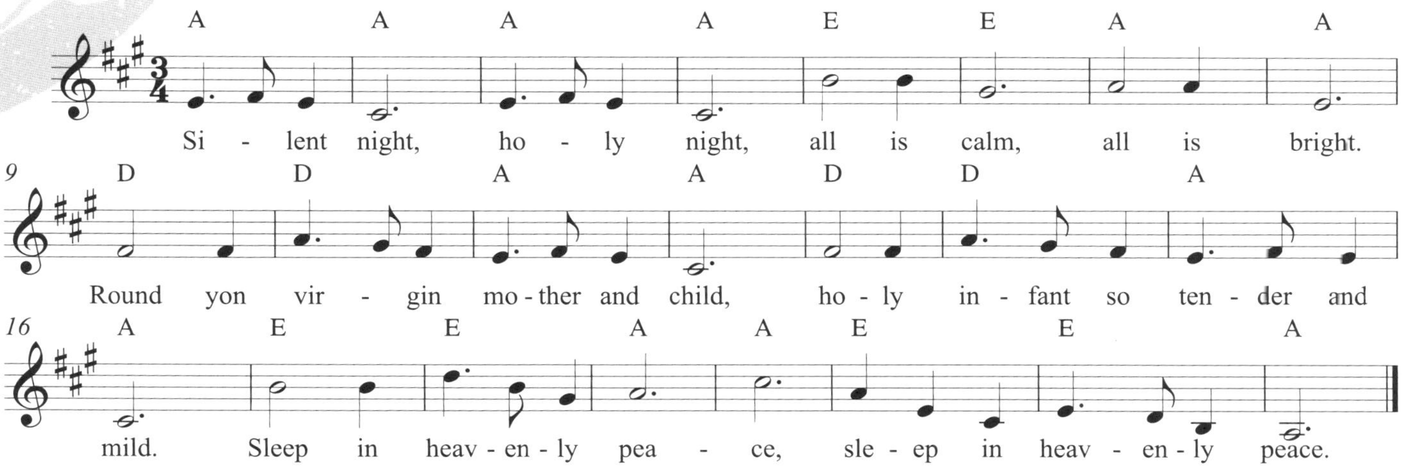

6 Frere Jaques

7 She'll be coming round the mountain

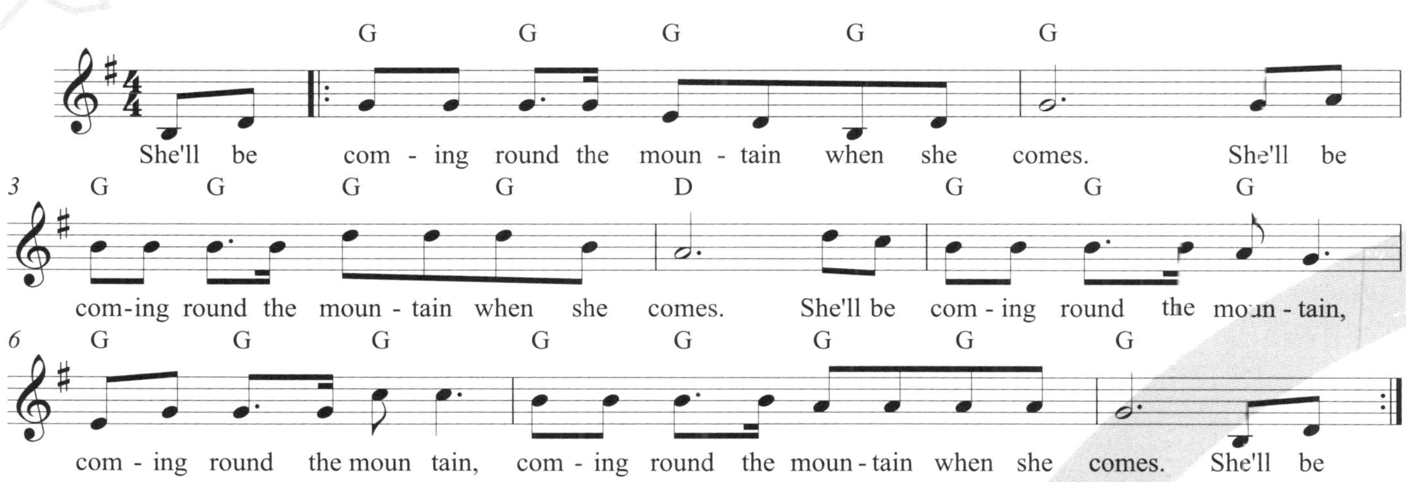

8 What will we do with the drunken sailor?

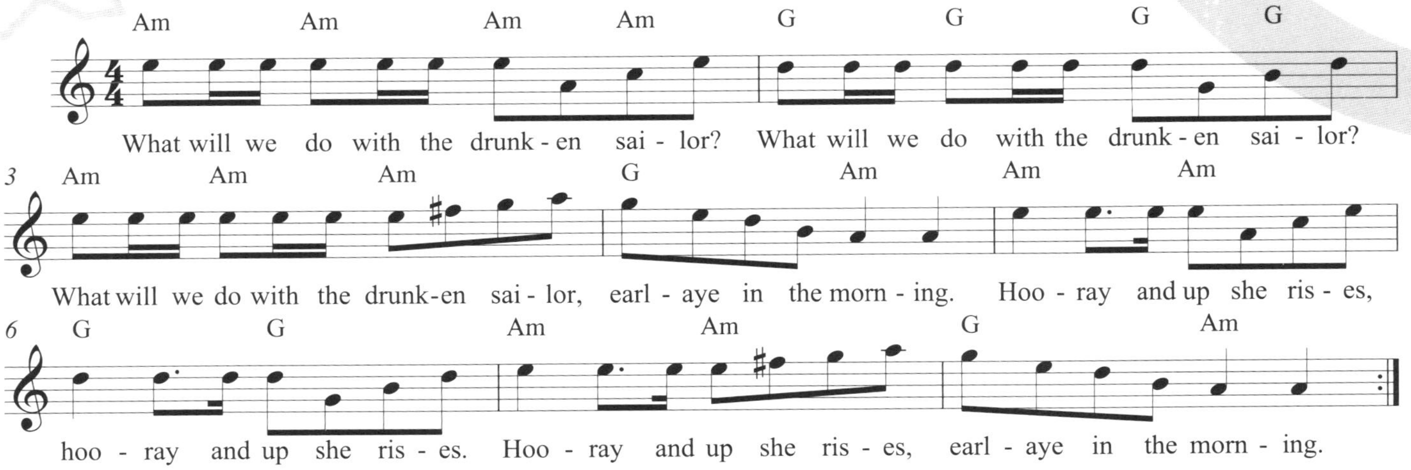

9 Away in a manger

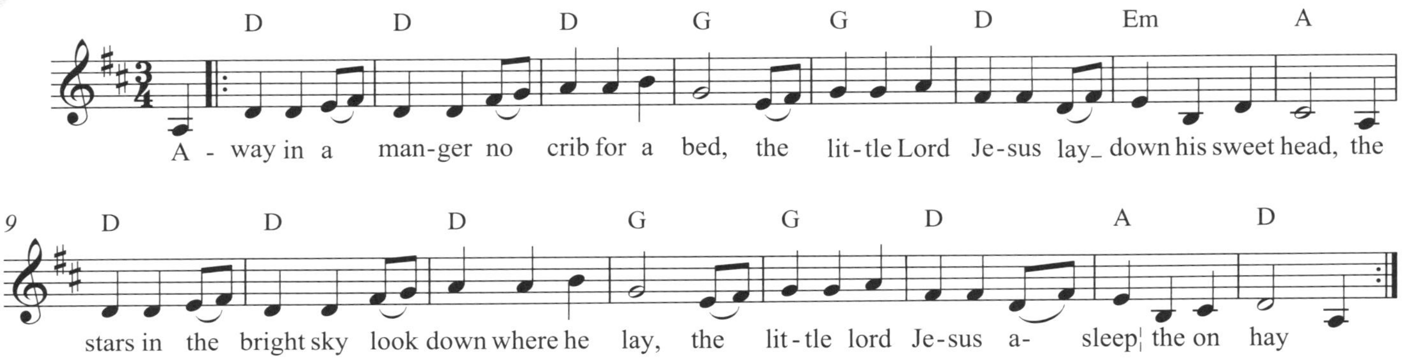

10 Wild thing

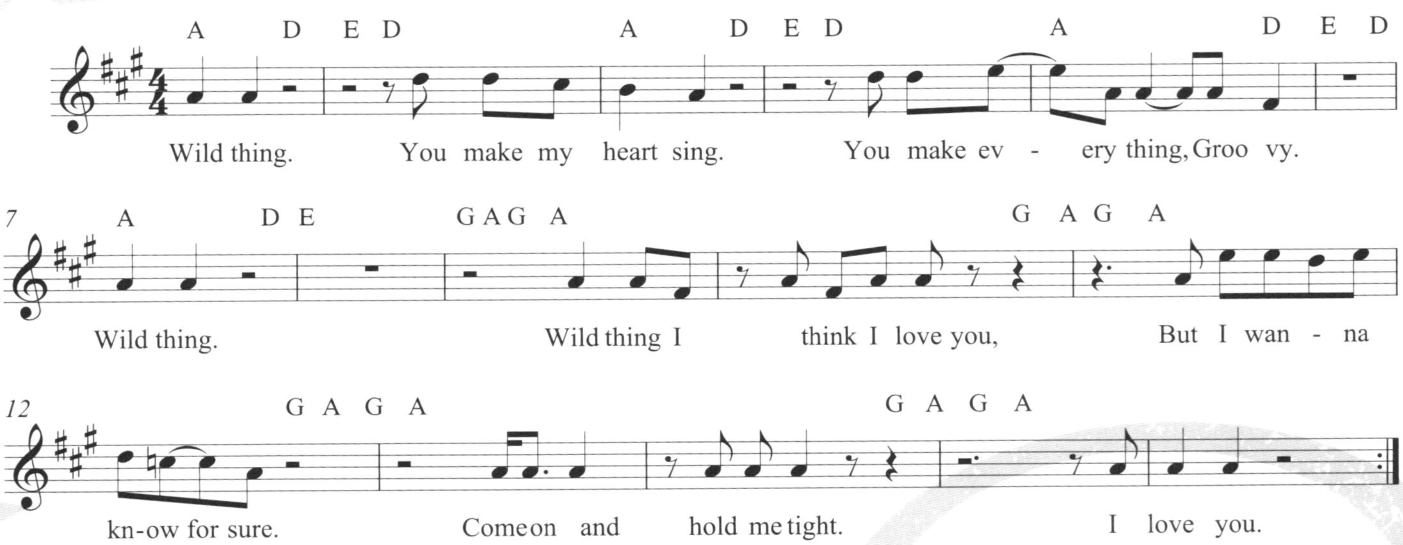

11 Little brown jug

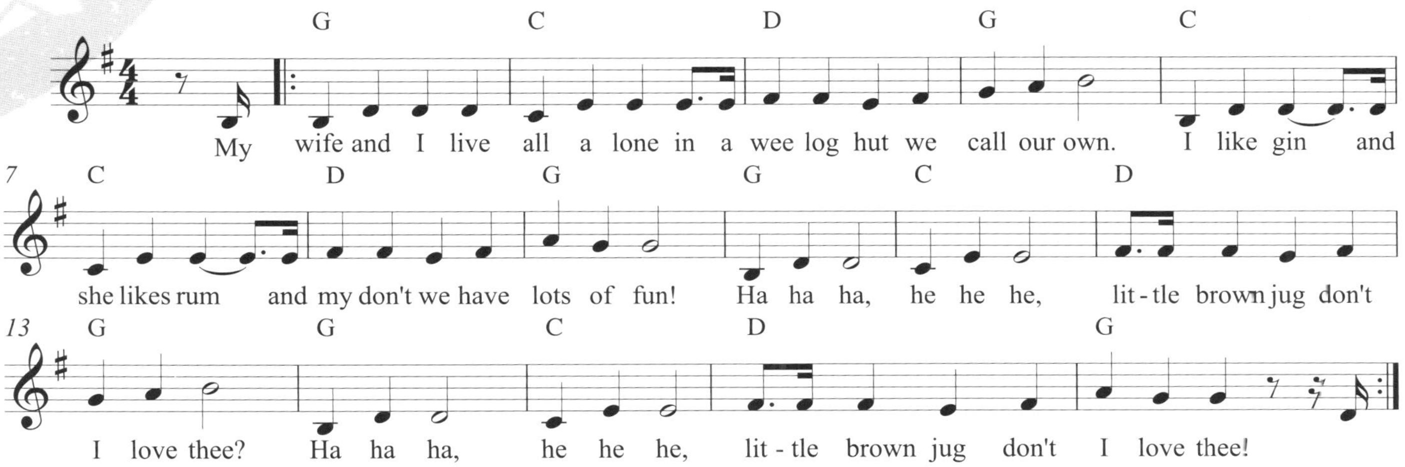

12 Rock around the clock

13 The animals went in two by two

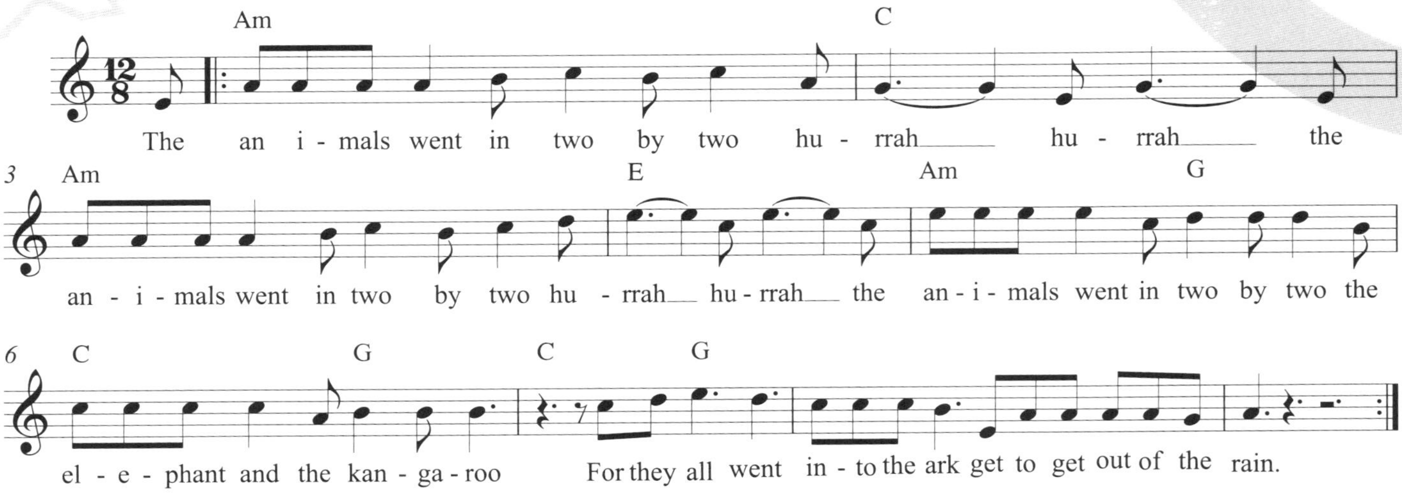

14 Amazing Grace

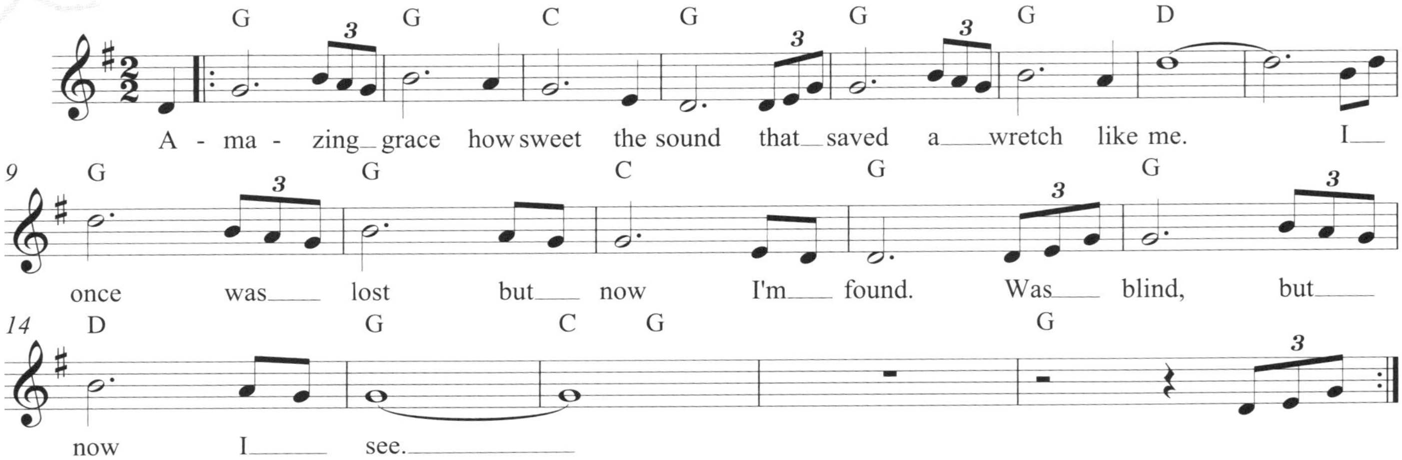

15 You really got me

16 Scarborough Fayre

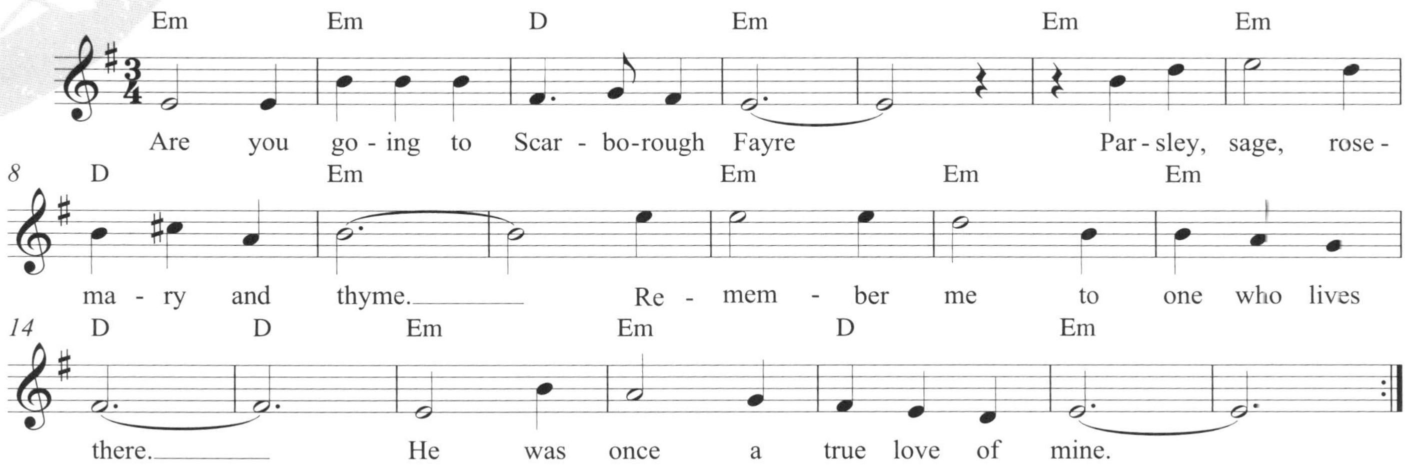

17 Head, shoulders, knees and toes

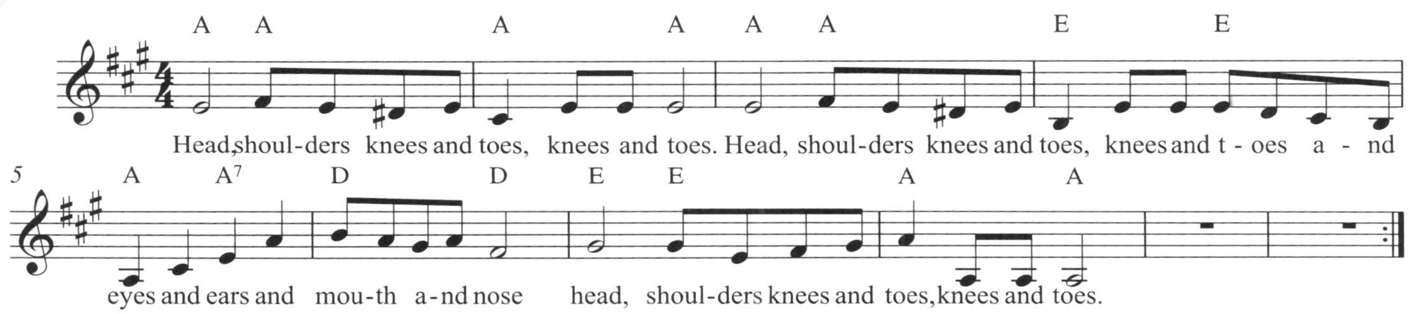

18 If you're happy and you know it

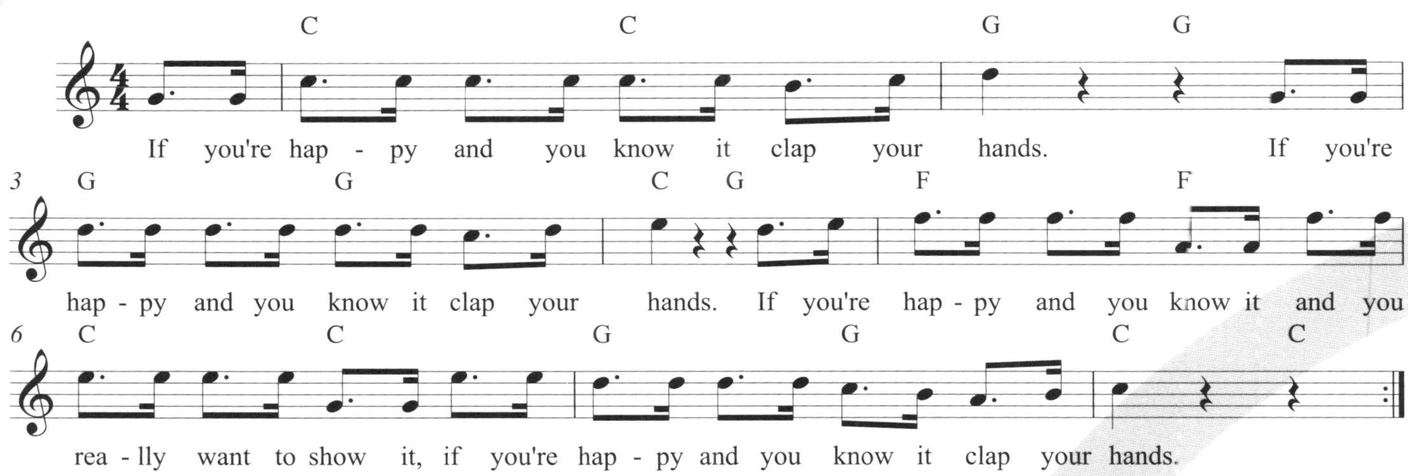

19 Jingle bells

20 Oh, when the saints go marching in

21 You are my sunshine

22 The House of the rising sun

23 Daisy Bell

24 My Bonnie lies over the ocean

25 I can see clearly now the rain is gone

Chord Index

A major

A

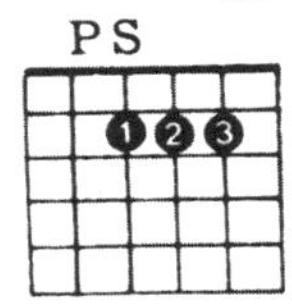

A7

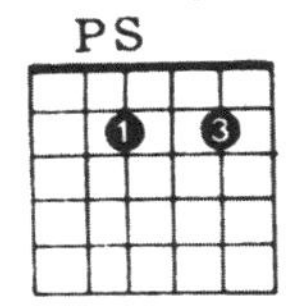

A minor

Am

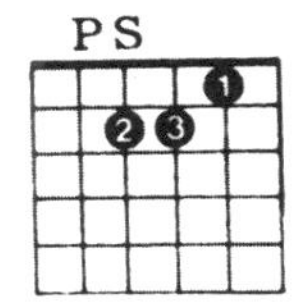

Am7

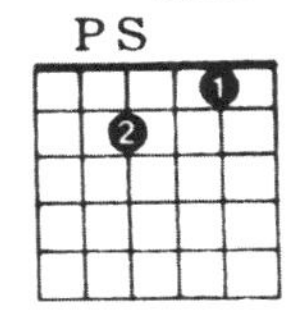

B♭ major (A♯ major)

B♭

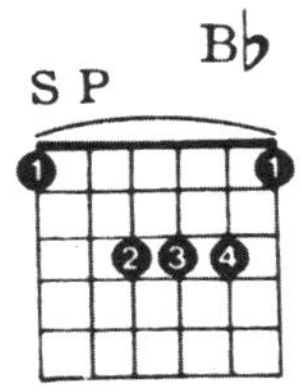

B♭7

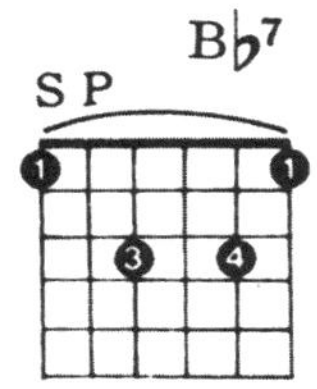

B♭ minor (A♯ minor)

B♭m

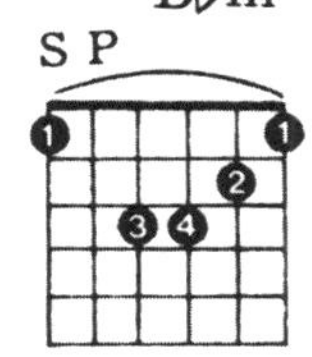

B♭m7

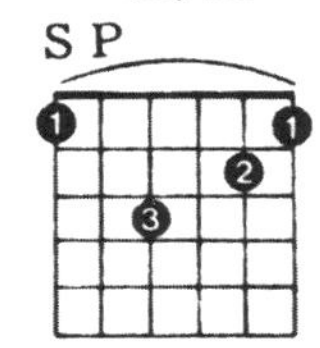

B major

B

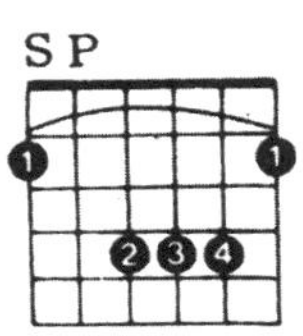

B7

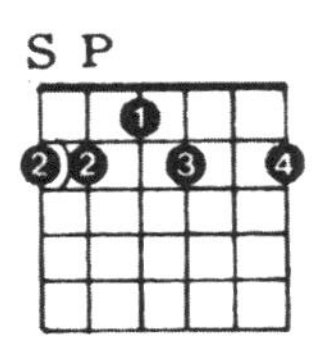

B minor

Bm

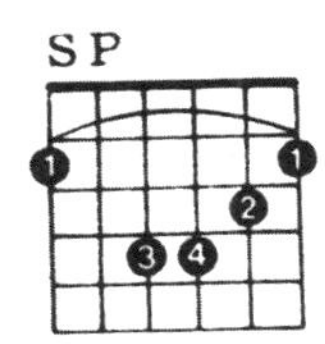

Bm7

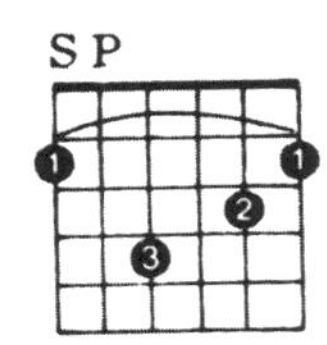

C major

C

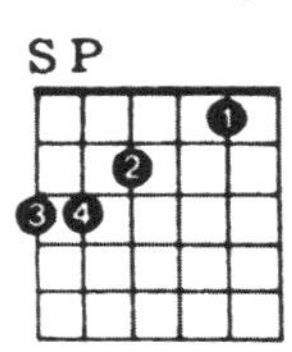

C7

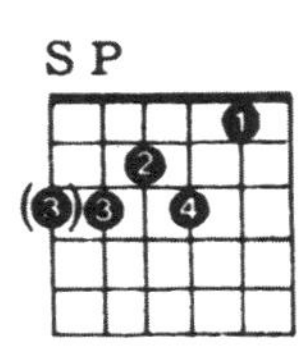

C minor

Cm

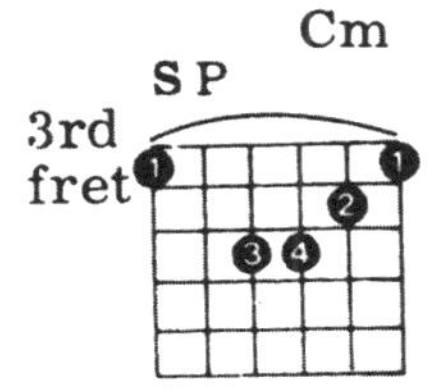

Cm7

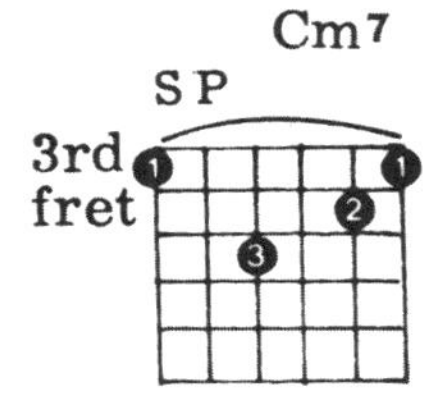

D♭ major (C♯ major)

D♭

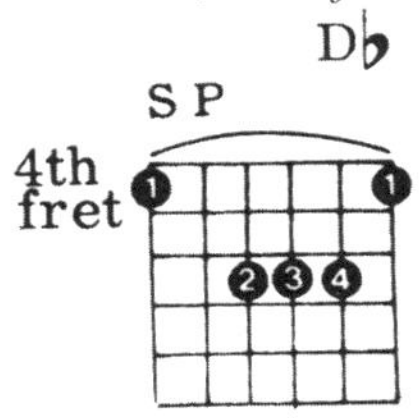

D♭7

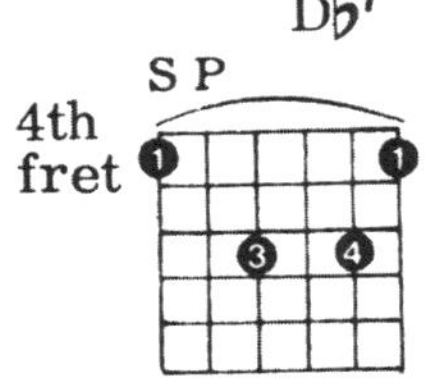

D♭ minor (C♯ minor)

D♭m

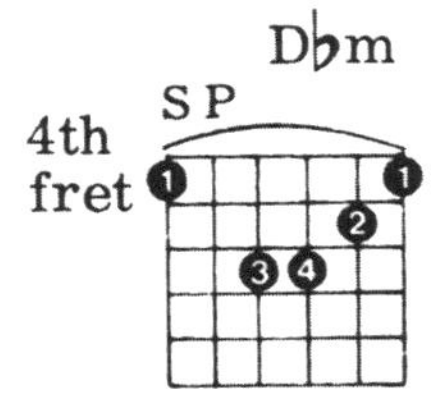

D♭m7

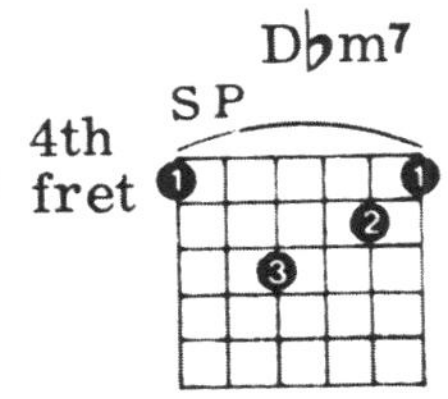

D major

D

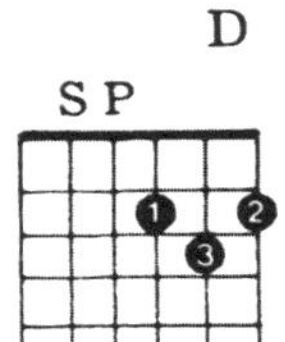

D7

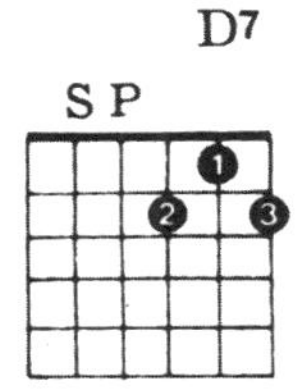

D minor

Dm

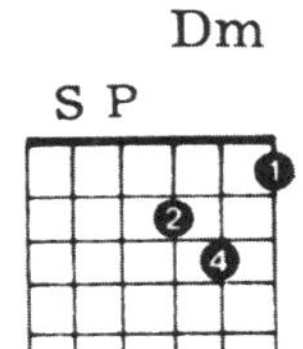

Dm7

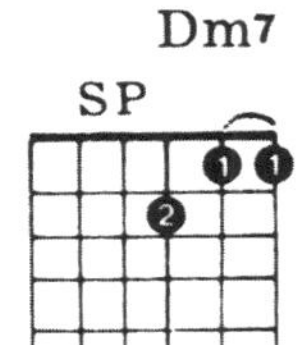

Chord Index

E♭

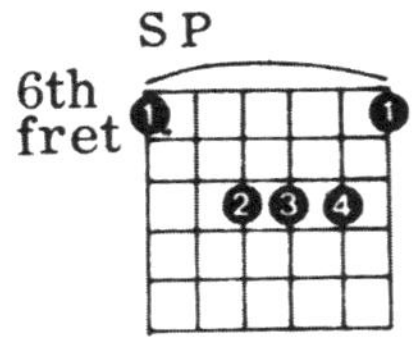

E♭7

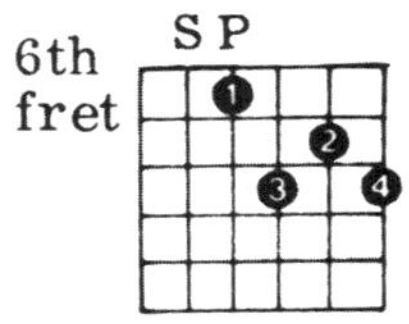

E♭m

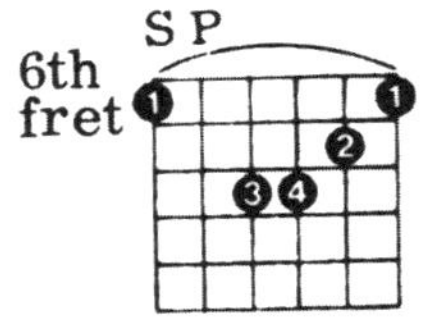

E♭m7

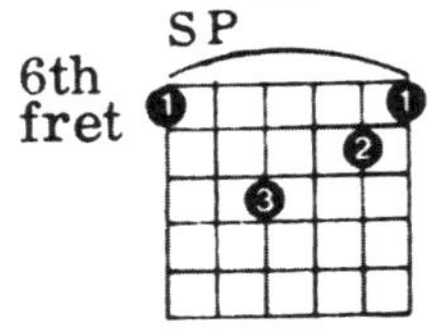

E major

E

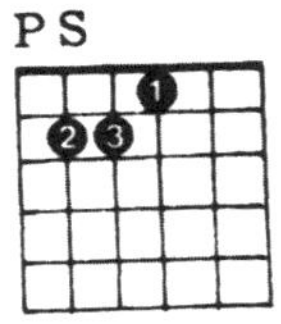

E7

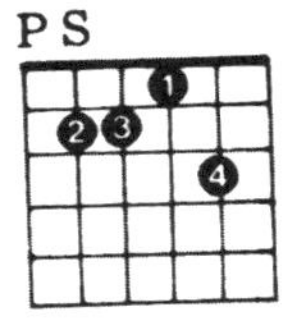

E minor

Em

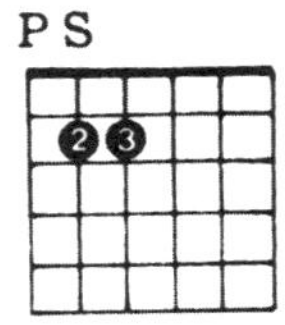

Em7

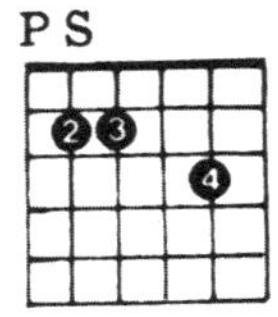

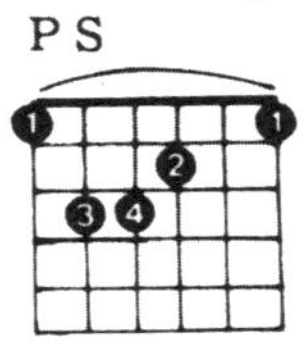

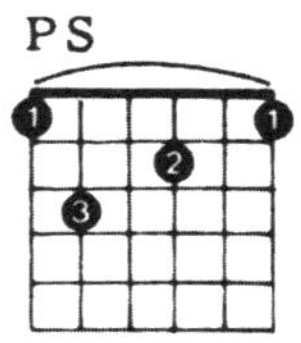

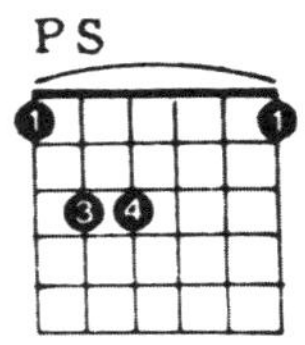

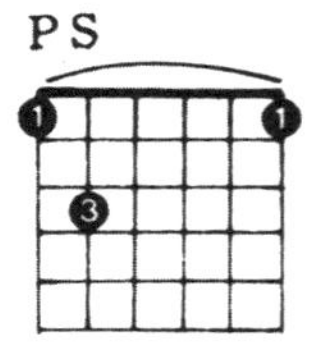

G♭ major (F♯ major)

G♭

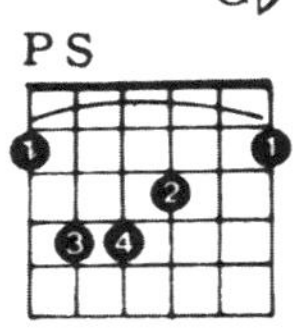

G♭7

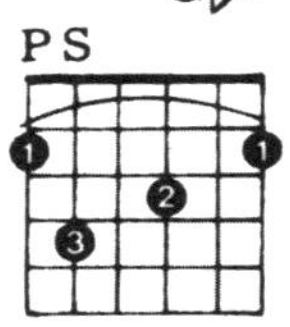

G♭ minor (F♯ minor)

G♭m

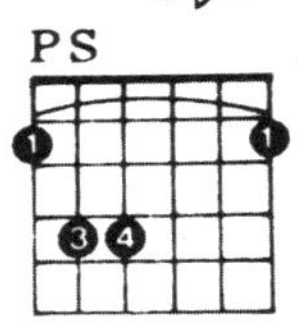

G♭m7

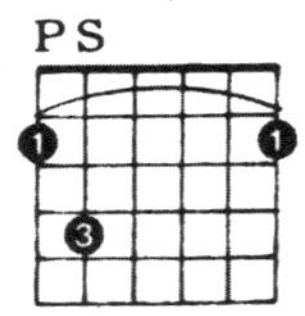

G major

G

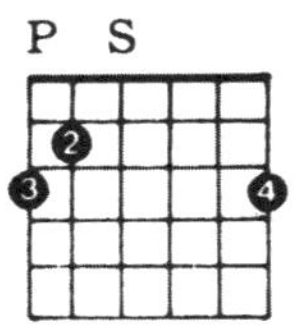

G7

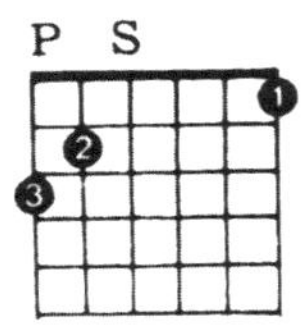

G minor

Gm

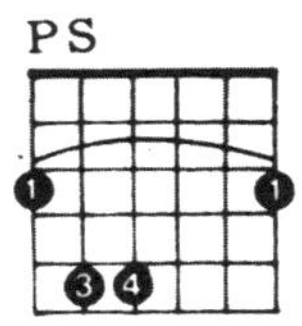

Gm7

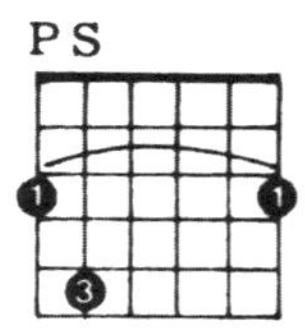

A♭ major (G♯ major)

A♭

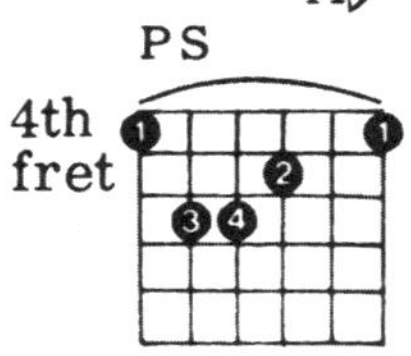

A♭7

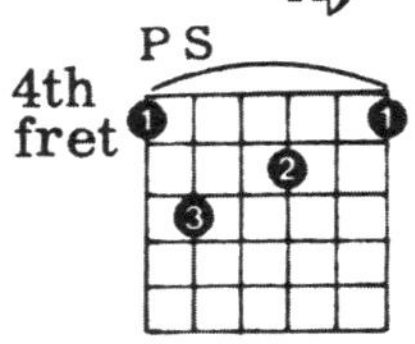

A♭ minor (G♯ minor)

A♭m

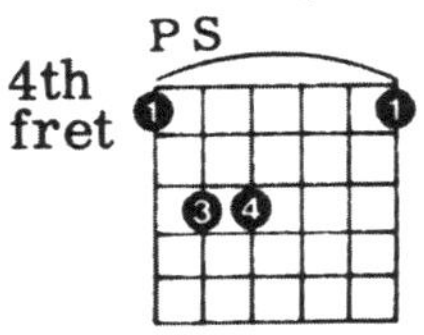

A♭m7

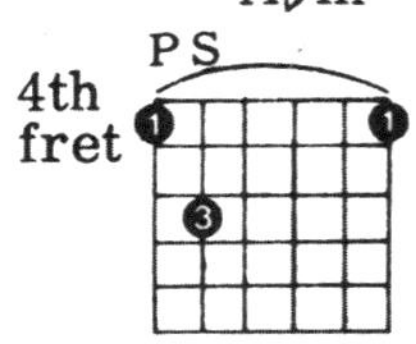